Investing in Stock Markets

Investing in Stock Markets

By

Anil R. Chougule
Associate Professor,
Department of Business Economics,
Sydenham College of Commerce and Economics,
Mumbai

New Century Publications
New Delhi, India

NEW CENTURY PUBLICATIONS
4852 / 24, 1st Floor,
Ansari Road, Daryaganj,
New Delhi – 110 002 (India)

Tel.: 011-4101 7798; 4358 7398; 98112 66355
E-mail: info@newcenturypublications.com

www.newcenturypublications.com

Editorial office:
4800 / 24, Bharat Ram Road,
Ansari Road, Daryaganj,
New Delhi – 110 002

First Published: **2022**

ISBN: **978-81-7708-542-6**

Published by New Century Publications and printed at Milan Enterprises, New Delhi.

Designs: Patch Creative Unit, New Delhi.

PRINTED IN INDIA

About the Book

A stock (or share) market is an integral part of a modern financial system. Stock market is a platform for making investment in corporate securities. The securities are chiefly in the form of equity shares and debentures. The purpose of these securities is to raise long-term funds for companies engaged in production. The function of a stock market is two-fold: (a) to arrange for the raising of new capital (primary market function) and (b) to provide liquidity against existing securities (secondary market function). Corporate enterprises raising fresh capital may be new companies or existing companies planning expansion of their operations. Sometimes, existing private firms also go public, i.e. become public limited companies.

Stock market helps in the floatation of new issues by providing a variety of services like underwriting, distribution, and listing of the issue. Stock market contributes in raising capital in order to strengthen the industrial base of an economy. Thus, stock market plays an most important role in supporting the growth of industry and commerce in the country.

Ever since the initiation of economic reforms in the early 1990s, the Indian stock market has undergone a sea change. Development of information technology in general and digital technology in particular, has changed the approach of people towards the stock market. As a chief regulator, Securities and Exchange Board of India (SEBI) has brought transparency along with friendly access for investors across the country. Indian stock market is also an attraction for foreign portfolio investors.

This book explains and examines various aspects of stock market in India. It is designed to help a cross-section of readers—particularly teachers and students of economics, commerce and management—to understand the intricacies of the functioning of Indian stock market in a non-technical language.

About the Author

Dr. Anil R. Chougule is presently working as Associate Professor, Department of Business Economics, Sydenham College of Commerce and Economics, Mumbai. He completed his Post-graduation, M.Phil. and Ph.D. from the Department of Economics, Shivaji University, Kolhapur. He specialises in finance and stock market. He has published a number of research papers in national and international journals of repute. With more than 17 years of teaching experience to graduate and post-graduate students, he is a member of board of studies of various universities and autonomous colleges.

Dr. Chougule has participated and presented papers at various national and international conferences and seminars.

Contents

Preface

A well-developed stock market helps to access external capital which allows financially constrained domestic firms to expand. It is argued that countries with developed stock markets tend to grow faster.

Stock market in India has become modern and comparable to the best in the world in terms of market infrastructure, trading and settlement practices and risk management systems. However, given the size of the Indian economy, the capital raised from the securities market has remained quite small. Companies, by and large, tend to finance their investment activities through alternative sources, which have inhibited the growth of the market. Large and well-known companies in India have tended to prefer international capital markets. Huge resources have also been raised by way of debt issues from the private placement market, which is less cumbersome, fast and economical. However, this segment lacks transparency and appears to be growing at the expense of the public issues segment. Lack of sufficient capital market activity has hindered the process of diversification of investment from fixed income instruments to equity-based instruments by the households.

The stock market helps the floatation of new issues by providing a variety of services like underwriting, distribution, and listing of the issue. Underwriting means guaranteeing the purchase of a fixed amount of new issues by the underwriter. The new issues of capital may be a public issue or a rights issue or both in certain proportions. It may be in the form of equity shares or debentures. Debentures, in turn, may be fully convertible, partly convertible, or non-convertible into shares. A public issue implies that the general public is invited to subscribe to the new issue. A rights issue is restricted for subscription by existing shareholders.

There is a need to ensure that the corporates are able to raise resources from the capital market in a timely and cost-effective manner. The need is also felt to develop strong domestic institutional investors, which would serve many purposes.

As the market evolution is an ongoing process, the Indian equity market would have to continuously strive to keep up to the international standards. In particular, corporate governance practices need to be strengthened further to raise the confidence level of a common investor. This would also enhance flow of institutional money to equities.

Acknowledgements

It gives me immense pleasure to express my gratefulness to those who helped me in this endeavour. I am indebted to Professor (Dr.) Ramesh R. Dandage, formerly Professor, Department of Economics, Shivaji University, Kolhapur and Professor (Dr.) Vidhya Katti, Department of Economics, Shivaji University Kolhapur who have been a constant source of encouragement and inspiration for me. I put on record my sincere thanks to Dr. Madhuri Kagalkar, Principal, Sydenham College of Commerce and Economics, Mumbai for her kind help and support.

Thanks are also due to my colleagues and well-wishers, in particular, Dr. Ranu Jain, Dr. Khushpat Jain, Dr. Ritesh Singhal, Dr. Abhay Khamborkar, Professor Rajendra Mali, Dr. Jharna Kalra and Shri Unmesh Nangare.

I also take this opportunity to express my gratitude and affection for my family members including my grandmother Shrimati Parvati Chougule, uncle Shri B.T. Chougule, father-in-law Shri Ananda Patil, sister Shobha and brother Yuvraj. My wife Anuradha, daughter Srushti and son Jay deserve special mention for giving me moral support at every stage of this academic pursuit.

Mumbai **Anil R. Chougule**
July 2022

Abbreviations/Acronyms

ADR	American Depository Receipt
ASBA	Applications Supported by Blocked Amount
AUM	Asset Under Management
BOLT	BSE's Online Trading System
BSE	Bombay Stock Exchange
CAPM	Capital Asset Pricing Model
CARE	Credit Analysis and Research Ltd.
CRA	Credit Rating Agency
CDSL	Central Depository Services (India) Ltd.
CGR	Compound Growth Rate
CIV	Collective Investment Vehicles
CRA	Central Record Keeping Agency
CRISIL	Credit Rating Information Services of India Limited
CTT	Commodities Transaction Tax
DCA	Department of Company Affairs
DCF	Discounted Cash Flow
DEA	Department of Economic Affairs
DHRF	Draft Red Herring Prospectus
DMA	Direct Market Access
DMA	Day Moving Average
DR	Depository Receipt
DRHP	Draft of Red Herring Prospectus
ELSS	Equity Linked Savings Scheme
EMH	Efficient Market Hypothesis
EPS	Earnings Per Share
ETF	Exchange Traded Fund
F&O	Future and Options
FDI	Foreign Direct Investment
FERA	Foreign Exchange Regulation Act
FIIs	Foreign Institutional Investors
FPIs	Foreign Portfolio Investors
GDR	Global Depository Receipt
GNI	Gross National Income

GoI	Government of India
GST	Goods and Services Tax
ICDR	Issue of Capital and Disclosure Requirements
ICRA	Investment Information and Credit Rating Agency of India Ltd.
IDBI	Industrial Development Bank of India
IDRs	Indian Depository Receipts
IPO	Initial Public Offer
IRDA	Insurance Regulatory and Development Authority of India
IRR	India Rating and Research Pvt. Ltd.
ISC	International Securities Consultancy
MACD	Moving Average Convergence Divergence
MCX	Multi Commodity Exchange
NASDAQ	National Association of Securities Dealers Automated Quotations
NAV	Net Asset Value
NCDEX	National Commodity and Derivatives Exchange
NIM	New Issue Market
NSCC	National Securities Clearing Corporation
NSDL	National Securities Depository Ltd.
NSE	National Stock Exchange
NSSA	Native Share and Stockbrokers Association
NTPC	National Thermal Power Corporation
NYSE	New York Stock Exchange
OTCEI	Over the Counter Exchange of India
PAN	Permanent Account Number
PIS	Portfolio Investment Scheme
PMLA	Prevention of Money Laundering Act
QIB	Qualified Institutional Buyer
QIP	Qualified Institutional Placement
RBI	Reserve Bank of India
RET	Rational Expectations Theory
RFDs	Ready Forward Deals
RGESS	Rajiv Gandhi Equity Saving Scheme

RHP	Red Herring Prospectus
ROE	Return on Equity Ratio
RSI	Relative Strength Index
S&P	Standard & Poor's
SAT	Securities Appellate Tribunal
SEBI	Securities and Exchange Board of India
SGF	Settlement Guarantee Fund
SIP	Systematic Investment Plan
SLBS	Securities Lending and Borrowing Scheme
SLR	Statutory Liquidity Ratio
SMA	Simple Moving Average
SME	Small and Medium-Sized Enterprises
SMERA	Small and Medium Enterprises Rating Agency
SRO	Self-Regulatory Organization
STT	Securities Transaction Tax
TCS	Tata Consultancy Services
TOI	Times of India
UTI	Unit Trust of India
WDM	Wholesale Debt Market

1

Stock Market: Conceptual Framework

Stock market is a common feature of a modern economy. These days, it is not the only buzzword in business world but also attraction of the present generation. Stock market is also known as securities market, or share market. Generally, market of an economy is divided into three categories viz., product market, factor market and financial market. Stock market belongs to the financial market. A financial market channelizes funds from savers to companies and hence acts as a link between investors and the corporate sector. Share market is an organised financial market for industrial and government securities, where shares and debentures of different companies are bought and sold.

1.1 Role of Stock Market in Economic Development

Stock market contributes in raising capital in order to strengthen the industrial base of an economy. Thus, stock market plays an important role in supporting the growth of industry and commerce in a country.

For the developed countries, stock market is a barometer of country's economy. A rising stock market is sign of a developing industrial and corporate sector and an indication of growing economy of the country. The performance of stock market, directly and indirectly, is affected by the economic decisions of the country.

Like product market, stock market involves buyers and sellers in which shares of listed companies are traded. Stock market provides a platform to the holders of securities to exchange their securities with the potential buyers for money or money's worth. Although, the behaviour of buyers and sellers in this market is highly unpredictable, various theories and models such as fundamental analysis and technical analysis help in predicting likely movements in the market over a period of time.

Stock market is a platform for making investments in high risk and high return securities, that involves certain stages i.e. come, watch, buy, wait, sell and exit. If stock halts at any of these stages for a longer period than expected, a buyer/seller may suffer losses because every stage contains a specific time value for profit making. At the same time, if the investor halts at any of these stages, his likelihood of making losses increases. Stock market is information sensitive. Buyers and sellers are fully aware of the market situations.

Stock market is a liquid market in which securities can be readily converted into cash. Stock market is made up of four major components, namely, buyers, sellers, shares and regulators.

Stock market is not a gambling tank. It is necessary and an integral part of the present economic scenario. Thus, stock exchange is really an essential pillar of the private sector corporate economy. Finance minister of India Mr. C.D. Deshmukh while placing Security Contracts (Regulation) Bill in November 1958 stated that economic services which a well constituted and efficiently run securities market can render to a country with large private sector under normal incentives and impulses of private enterprises are considerable. "In first place, it is only an organised security market which can provide sufficient marketability and price continuity for shares necessary for investors. Secondly, it is only such a market that can provide a reasonable measure of safety and fair dealing in buying and selling of securities. Thirdly, through the interplay of demand and supply of securities, a proper organised stock exchange, assists in a reasonably correct evaluation of securities in term of their real worth. Lastly, through such evaluation of securities, stock exchange helps in the orderly flow of distribution of savings between different types of competitive instruments". [1]

Role of stock market in economic development is associated

with primary and secondary market. Economic development depends on industrial development. Industrial development is correlated to capital formation, and capital formation depends on mobilisation of savings. Stock market is an open auction market where facility is available to raise capital for expansion through selling of shares to the investing public of firms interested in their further expansion.

These days, capital intensive companies, particularly high tech companies, constantly are in need to raise high amount of capital in their early stages of business. In this respect, stock exchange, which is a public market platform, has been one of the most important funding sources for many capital intensive start-ups.

When people invest in shares through an initial public offering (IPO) or in secondary market, it usually leads to rational allocation of resources. It is not only helping the companies' management boards to finance their organizations, but also promotes business activity with benefits for several economic sectors.

To sum up, stock exchanges have contributed significantly to the growth and expansion of national business; it ultimately promotes well-being of the national economy and its people. Stock market through IPO and stock exchanges provide an ideal channel through which huge amount of capital flow is channelized for productive purposes. Stock market has been assuring the owners of corporate securities to sell their securities at any time and in a way, provides liquidity. Thus, share market provides the most common platform for business entities to grow by acquisition or fusion. A stock exchange indicates the state of health of companies and national economy, and hence, stock index is one of the economic barometers of a country's development.

1.2 Characteristics of Stock Market

1.2.1 Larger Number of Buyers and Sellers: In a perfectly competitive market, there are large number of buyers and sellers. Similarly, in a stock market also, there are number of buyers and sellers.

Large number of buyers and sellers ensure that purchase or sale by any one individual buyer or seller will not affect the market price. Each buyer or seller buy or sell a relatively small fraction of the total market supply and therefore, is not capable of exerting any perceptible influence on the market. Therefore, each buyer and seller is a price taker and not price maker. This is true not only in case of a perfectly competitive market, but also true in case of a stock market as stock market also consists of large institutional buyers like FIIs, HNIs, pension funds, mutual funds, banks, insurance companies, etc. The volume of purchase and sale of these institutional buyers in the market is so high that their actions do exercise a significant influence on market prices.

Critics often view price trends on major stock markets in the world as a result of collusion among large buyers and sellers. But this possibility is low as the stock market is spread over the entire world. Yet, there are many instances of collusion at the local level in major stock markets of the world, including India.

1.2.2 Homogenous Product: The second important feature of perfectly competitive market is that the products in such markets are homogeneous in nature in terms of size, shape, colour, quality, etc. Similarly, the nature of commodity (i.e., shares and securities) that are traded in stock market, is homogeneous. Shares and securities that deal in the stock market derive their value from the performance of the company to which they belong to. Therefore, all shares and securities of the same company have same worth across all markets. In other words, the product is not differentiated. Therefore, a buyer can buy a stock from any seller and/or broker.

1.2.3 High Degree of Substitutability: As the products sold in a perfectly competitive market are homogenous in nature, they are perfect substitutes of each other. Securities of various competitive companies from the same industry are listed on the stock market. Therefore, a buyer has a wide range of options to choose from in the stock market. The various scrips bought and sold in the stock market possess a high degree of substitutability, which ensures a measure of homogeneity. The buyer has freedom to choose from a variety of securities, which are close substitute for each other. Therefore, cross-elasticity of demand for shares and securities in the stock market is high.

1.2.4 Perfect Information: Perfect information is a situation that arises, when information about prices and quantities is readily available. In a perfectly competitive market, each buyer and seller has complete knowledge about the market conditions. In stock market too, everyone has free and equal access to information about prices and quantities traded. Buyers and sellers are constantly informed about the price and quantity of stocks traded on the stock market through various official websites like BSE, NSE, Moneycontrol.com, etc. In addition to that, there are various private agencies which constantly collect information about various sectors, companies, government policies and changes in national and international economic environment to help predict movements in the stock market. The price and trading in stock market are extremely sensitive to market information.

1.2.5 Freedom of Entry and Exit: In a perfectly competitive market, there is no barrier to entry and exit. Similarly, in a stock market, buyers and sellers are free to enter the market or exit from market at any point of time without any restriction. Stock market is regulated by the regulators. Every player in the market has to follow the rules and regulations designed by regulators. When there is a boom in the market, many new players enter the market. Similarly, when there is a slump in the market many of them leave the market. But, the entry of an individual in a stock market is subject to his financial capacity. In some cases, exit is restricted in terms of time, commonly known as the lock-in period.

1.2.6 Reserve Price: Wicksteedian concept of reservation price is more applicable to the sellers in the stock market than sellers in any other markets. Reserve price means the highest price beyond which a buyer is not going to buy a stock or the smallest price below which a seller is not going to sell a stock. Thus, a transaction in a particular stock will be struck between any of these two reserve prices.

The market for securities being predominantly a secondary market, the volume of existing securities and minimum reserve price of the sellers and the buyers have an important bearing on the supply of securities in the market at any given point of time.

1.2.7 Independence in Price Changes: Independence in price is a distinctive feature of a highly perfect market. Prices of securities are highly unpredictable and do not rely on any specific factor.

One cannot anticipate price changes exclusively on the basis of behaviour of prices in the past. Price follows a random course in the stock market. Information on the future prospects is frequently received and widely and quickly disseminated in stock market and the prices in the stock market adjust instantaneously to such new information. A gradual adjustment of prices to new information would create trends in price series. Thus, stock prices are independent with respect to time, that is, past prices.

1.2.8 Continuous Market and Continuity: Stock market provides a liquid and continuous market for securities, where investors can convert their money into securities and securities into money quickly during the trading hours by making bids and offers, as it is an open auction, where buyers and sellers compete with each other. This enables prices of shares and securities to find their *true and fair* market on the basis of demand and supply. The free-market mechanism provides marketability, stability and continuity in the prices. It facilitates the transfer of ownership of securities from one person/entity to another and reduces the risk of investors.

1.2.9 Transaction Cost: The cost of doing transactions in the stock market is referred to as the impact cost. In stock market, transaction cost is incurred at various stages of transaction of securities viz. trading, clearing and settlement, etc. Few examples of transaction cost include, brokerage, stamp duty, fees to intermediaries, securities transaction tax (STT) etc.

1.2.10 Speculation/Speculative Transaction: This is one of the important features of a stock market. Speculation is an inspiration that makes stock market more alive. Speculation is the purchase or sale of securities, with the object of making profit from a short period variation in market prices. In this activity, the normal practice is to square up transactions by offsetting a sale (purchase) by purchase (sale). Only differences in prices are paid, and the delivery of securities and payment of full price are very rare. However, speculation is not gambling.

In the absence of speculation, demand and supply may not be equal and therefore, may not lead to violent price fluctuations. For instance, if demand is extremely higher than supply, the price will shoot up and vice-versa. Thus, speculators promote demand and supply equilibrium, and stability of prices.

In stock market, speculators are classified as bulls, bears, stags and lame ducks.

1.2.11 Highly Volatile Market: This basically means that stock market is a changeable market—volatility is a measure of the risk in financial instrument. Volatility refers to the relative rate at which the price of a security moves up and down. Volatility is calculated by the daily or annualised standard deviation of daily changes in stock price. In stock market, one can earn money, but there are equal chances of incurring losses. Sometimes, people meet with the losses higher than the profit.

1.2.12 Manipulation: In this case, speculators manipulate the market through unfair practices, like spreading false rumours or by giving wrong and misleading information, to make profit for themselves at the expense of general investors. Manipulative activities include options, wash sales, touting, inside collusion, manipulation of fundamentals, and corners. The purpose of manipulation is to push up demand for any particular securities in an improper way and thus, push up the prices of securities. Option means that speculators protect them from risk and loss. Wash sales mean transactions by the manipulators involving themselves. Touting refers to disseminating tips and rumours. Manipulation of fundamentals refers to illegal practices of directors and top officials of companies to manipulate earnings. Corners means buying of a large portion of a company's shares by a party with the intent to push up its prices.

1.2.13 Supply and Demand Elasticity in Stock Market: In stock market, the stock prices are very sensitive to various economic and non-economic factors. Thus, demand and supply of shares in stock market are highly elastic, i.e. a small increase in price of a share will decrease demand for the share and will increase its supply and vice-versa.

Cross-elasticity of demand for shares in stock market is very high, i.e. when the price of any particular share rises exorbitantly, the demand for substitute stocks increases. For example, if the price of Infosys increases, the investors turn to invest in other substitute stocks like Wipro.

1.2.14 Factors Driving Demand in Stock Market: The forces on demand side for stocks are more complex and varied. In general, three motives govern an investor's decision to buy a particular security. These are safety, profitability and scope for capital appreciation. A buyer's decision to go in for scrip, therefore, depends on his relative evaluation and importance of these three qualities possessed by a stock. Investor's investment motives, thus, have a decisive influence on demand schedule for securities. A change in demand schedule for a security would, therefore, occur whenever a qualitative change happens, i.e. technical and fundamental factors in the stock market parlance. The technical factors relate to the internal organisation and structure of market. The fundamental factors refer to general business and growth prospect of the economy.

Besides these, qualitative changes regards the relative preferences of people in the market about holding liquid cash is a significant factor as well.

1.2.15 Short Selling: Short-selling is an important feature of the stock market. It is not just for providing liquidity, but also about helping price corrections in overvalued stocks. It is this practice, where investors sell their shares that they do not own at the time of selling. They sell them in the hope that the price of those shares will decline, and they will make profit by buying back those shares at a lower price. At present, there is no prohibition on short selling by retail investors in India. Equity short selling is allowed only intraday. Future and option positions in short selling can be carried over till expiry.

1.2.16 Role of Depositories: There are two depositories in the country, namely National Securities Depository Ltd. (NSDL) and Central Depository Services (India) Ltd. (CDSL). These are the only depositories in the Indian stock market. These depositories' deal with processing of shares traded and transfer them electronically without involving share certificates and transfer deeds, thus, eliminating the paper work involved in scrip-based trading and share transfer system. In short, transfer of shares held in dematerialised form takes place freely through electronic book-entry system.

1.2.17 Margin Trading System: It is an important feature of a stock market, which is quite different from other markets. It refers to the process whereby, an individual investor is able to buy more stock than they can afford. Margin trading also refers to intra-day trading in India. Stock brokers provide this service to investors. It requires opening a margin account with a broker. The broker will lend money to buy shares and keep them as collateral. In margin trading, one can borrow money from a broker to buy securities, while in short selling one can borrow securities to sell them. In both the cases, the investor is borrowing from the broker. Therefore, the only difference between margin trading and short selling is two forms of loans, i.e. either securities or cash only.

1.2.18 Limit Up and Limit Down Mechanism: In stock market, there is a provision of automatic circuit breakers or mandatory trading interruptions. It not only moderates extreme and unwarranted market price movements but also calms the stock market. Thus, circuit breakers promote price discovery process and builds investor confidence and trust, in the stock market.

1.2.19 Sector-wise Trend: The Indian securities market is broadly divided into various sectors that serve as broad categories for listed companies. There are about 11 diverse sectors listed in the Indian stock market, such as: financial, health care, IT, energy, real estate, utilities, communication, materials, and consumer staples. Generally, sectoral trends are observed in stock price movements. The stock exchange separately calculates index for different sectors such as Nifty IT index, Nifty Financial Services index, Nifty Reality index, Nifty Healthcare index etc. Once trade wave occurs in the industrial sector of an economy, it affects the entire sectors of stock market, either positively or negatively in anticipation of trade waves.

1.2.20 Organised Market: Stock market is an organised and regulated market. Generally, organised market means a market whose proceedings are governed by written rules and customs. Stock exchanges have management committees and are regulated by the Securities and Exchange Board of India (SEBI). All transactions take place as per the rules and regulations outlined by SEBI and management committees. It is a public market where only listed securities are traded. Investors can buy and sell securities in stock exchanges only through authorised members, called as brokers. While transacting in a stock exchange, every participant should obey the rules and by-laws determined by the stock exchanges and SEBI.

Price determination under stock market is classified into: short-run (daily stock prices) and long-run. The price of a particular stock is determined by its demand and supply in the stock market. A stock's price moves up and down during a day and is strictly the result of demand and supply. Supply is the number of shares offered for sale at any point of time. Demand is the number of shares investors wish to buy at exactly that point of time. Thus, supply equals the willing sellers and demand equals the willing buyers, where the mutual interest, is the current price.

If the buyers believe that company is not worth its current stock price, it will be manifest in a decrease in demand. If the seller realises that buyers are not willing to buy at the existing price, they will sell it to the available buyers at their price. This increases the supply, effectively pushing the price down. The reverse will happen if buyers believe the stock price is cheap and the sellers realize an increasing demand, effectively pushing up the price. Thus, interaction of demand and supply affects security prices every day in the stock market.

A stock market is always in one of the three states: First, it can be in a state, where demand exceeds supply, which means there is a competition to buy, leading to higher price. Second, it can be in a state, where supply exceeds demand, which means there is competition to sell, leading to a decline in price. Third, it can be in a state of equilibrium. At equilibrium, there is no competition to buy and sell. However, as the market moves away from equilibrium, competition increases which forces price back to equilibrium. In other words, competition eliminates itself by forcing market back to equilibrium. When demand and supply roughly equals, prices will bounce back and forth, but it narrows the price range. It is possible for a stock to stay in this range for days before something else disrupts the demand and supply balance.

Long-term price determination in a stock market is based on fundamental factors, which operate from outside the market like dividend policy, stock splits, general business conditions, condition in the labour market, growth prospects of the economy, industrial, fiscal and monetary policy of the government, market condition, and companies' strength and weakness.

1.3 Is Stock Market a Science or a Manipulation?

Well-known traditional saying is, "stock market is a gambling tank". Presently, there is mixed reaction of people about the stock market. Some say that it is a science, whereas some view it as a manipulated market. There are people who say that it is manipulated science or, stock market is manipulated scientifically.

Most of the successful traders and investors follow stock market as a science. Basically, science means a systematic body of knowledge. Its major characteristics are as under:

1. It is based on cause-and-effect relationship.
2. It is based on experiment.
3. It has a capacity to forecast.
4. Its rules are universally applicable.

Out of these four characteristics, fourth one is highly objectionable in social sciences. However, the study of stock market follows the first three characteristics. It is in fact a combination of art and science. There are two aspects of stock market investment: one is the fundamental analysis and the other is the technical analysis. Fundamental analysis is used for determining the potential of a company, whereas, technical analysis is used for predicting the future price movement of certain stocks. Technical analysis refers to historical facts and figures of stock market. Therefore, to become successful, investors have to follow these two aspects to earn good returns from the stock market.

Stock market is also manipulated like other markets. There are many examples of big scams in Indian capital market like the Harshad Mehta scam (1992), Ketan Parekh scam (2001) and the IPO scam. These scams occurred because the individuals were able to manipulate the system.

Can stock market be scientifically manipulated or not? It is a debatable question. Understanding investors' psychology is an art as well as a science. Stock market is not free from manipulation, but it may be manipulated for a short time or on a temporary basis. As market develops and implements new technology, manipulation goes on decreasing.

1.4 Investment versus Trading

Generally, *investment* and *trading* are used synonymously.

But in stock market these two terms are treated differently. Though the main aim of trading and investment is to earn profit, they are, however, attained in different ways. Investors have a long-term outlook while traders have a short-term outlook. Trading involves more frequent buying and selling of stocks, whereas the investment is often held for a longer period of time. There are different types of investment such as, gold, fixed deposits, real estate etc. According to J.M. Keynes, investment refers to real investment, that is, creation of income-earning assets.

Traders normally look at the price movement of stocks. In short, it is a skill of timing in the market. Investment is an art of creating wealth. Investment is compounding interest and dividend over the years by holding quality shares in the portfolio.

Both trading and investing carry risks. Yet, trading comparatively encompasses higher risk as compared to investment since trading is affected by many internal and external factors. Generally, the traders are skilled and technical individuals. Trading is related to the psychology of the market. Investors also analyse the stock which they want to purchase, but they focus on learning the business fundamentals.

Though investment and trading activities are treated differently in financial language, there is one common thing between them, i.e. trading and investment should be done wisely.

1.5 Stock Exchange: An Integral Part of the Stock Market

Stock exchange is an integral part of the stock market. There are number of definitions of stock exchanges, of which prominent ones are the following.

According to Pyle, "Stock exchanges are market places where securities *i.e.* shares, debentures, and bonds that have been listed thereon, may be bought and sold for either investment or speculation". [2]

According to the Securities Contracts (Regulation) Act, 1956, "Stock exchange means an association, organization or body of individuals whether incorporated or not, constituted for the purpose of assisting, regulating, or controlling the business of buying, selling or dealing in securities". [3]

According to Husband and Dockerary, "Stock exchanges are privately organized markets which are used to facilitate trading in securities". [4]

According to Cambell B. Harvey, "Stock market is a public market for trading of stocks and derivatives at an agreed price and also called the equity market, the market for trading equities". [5]

Stock exchange is a voluntary association managed by a governing body. The day-to-day administration is looked after by the governing board. All transactions of stock market are made through authorised members and brokers. Stock exchanges deal with second hand securities and money market instruments.

People desirous of converting their cash into securities can go to a stock exchange and buy securities with the help of brokers there. Similarly, securities can be converted into cash by selling them at the stock exchange.

To sum up, a stock (or share) market deals mainly in corporate securities. The securities are chiefly in the form of equity shares and debentures. The purpose of these securities is to raise long-term funds for companies engaged in production. The function of a stock market is two-fold: (a) to arrange for the raising of new capital (primary market function), and (b) to provide liquidity against existing securities (secondary market function). The new capital is raised through the issue of shares and debentures. The corporate enterprises raising new capital may be new companies or existing companies planning expansion of their operations. Sometimes, existing private firms go public, i.e. become public limited companies.

Stock market helps in floatation of new issues by providing a variety of services like underwriting, distribution, and listing of the issues. Transactions in the secondary market reflect investment climate in the economy. A well-developed stock market helps to access external capital which allows financially constrained domestic firms to expand. It is argued that countries with developed stock markets tend to grow faster.

Endnotes

1. K. Jadhav (1991), *Development of Capital Market in India*, A.J. Enterprises, pp. 53-54.
2. Ramesh Babu (2006), *Financial Market and Institutions*, Concept Publishing Company, New Delhi, p. 108.
3. The Securities Contracts (Regulation) Act, 1956, Section 2(3).
4. Krunal Mehta (2016), *Financial Market*, Sayone Publishing House, Rajkot, p. 47.
5. Ibid.

2

Theories of Stock Market

There are different theories followed in stock markets, namely, efficient market theory, rational theory and demand supply theory etc. Here, an attempt is being made to take a brief review of these theories related to stock market.

2.1 Efficient Market Hypothesis (EMH)

EMH was developed by Eugene Fama. It indicates the state of efficiency of the market. EMH is an investment theory that states it is impossible to "beat the market" because stock market efficiency causes existing share prices to always incorporate and reflect all relevant information. It can be also explained that if share prices are reflecting all accurate and available information of the relevant firms, which firms will be able to make a profit or the right production, and investors would be able to invest in the most appropriate firm. Accordingly, the market can be considered as an efficient market. Thus, efficiency is a state of affairs whereby the price in the security market reflects all the available information.

There are three degrees of the efficient market hypothesis: weak, semi-strong, and strong.

1. The weak form of EMH claims that past price movement data do not affect stock prices. The current stock prices reflect all the available information. The data of past price have no relationship with future direction of stock prices. Thus, the excess returns in stock market cannot be achieved using the technical analysis.
2. The semi-strong form of EHM implies that the market is efficient and reflects all publicly available information. It can be also interpreted that security prices reflect all new available information, and investors purchase securities

after this information is released. In this situation, excess returns in stock market cannot be achieved by using the fundamental analysis.

3. The strong form of the efficient market hypothesis means that current stock prices fully reflect all public and private information. No one has monopolistic access to the market information. It may be a situation of perfect market but no one investor would be able to earn profit above the average investor even if he was given the new information.

In an efficient market, the stocks are fairly priced. This means that there is no over valuation or under valuation of the stocks. Therefore, it is not possible in an efficient market to make excess or abnormal returns. The stock prices are equal to the fair value or fundamental value of the stocks. But it is empirically proved that most of stock markets in the world are not efficient, they are either in weak or semi-strong form of efficiency. Indian stock market belongs to the semi-weak form of market efficiency.

In short, EMH is based on the notion that people behave rationally. Although, most of analysts follow EMH yet, EMH is also criticised by financial experts on different grounds. The well-known figure in stock market Warren Buffett is exceptional to EMH and has consistently beaten the market over longer periods of time. According to him, "I find it is a waste of time for investors to worry about proving or disproving theories like EMH. Investing is an art, not a science. There are only theories, not absolute facts about how to invest". [1]

2.2 Expectations in Stock Market

Ideologically speaking, stock market is a platform of trust. Study of expectations is important for understanding stock markets. The consumers' expectations drive the market. Generally, consumer expectation with reference to the stock market refers to the economic needs and wants of individuals in the economy. These consumers' expectations can be studied in two ways: one, in the context of consumer expectations and industrial development, and second in the context of consumer expectations and stock market sentiments. During the period 2014 o 2019, the stock market index viz. 'Sensex' which was at 22,000 points in 2014 rallied up to 34,000 points in 2019. Though, it indicates the performance of our industrial sector, it is also the result of consumer expectations and investor sentiments. What will be the future of this rally? Of course with ups and downs, it will cross different milestones. What is the driving force behind it? The answer is expectations and sentiments of the investors.

As stated in the earlier paragraphs, consumer expectations and industrial development are inter-related (correlated) to each other. Consumer expectations are associated with life style. Looking at the life style, it is obvious that are day by day wants and needs are increasing. The materialist approach of life creates demand in the market, which is good for the development of the industrial sector. Industries are busy fulfilling consumer needs and wants, thereby bringing prosperity in the industrial sector. If our expectations are increasing with our progressive life style, then it motivates the industries to perform better. If industries perform well, then it is good for the stock market index, because stock market index reflects the performance of industries. Therefore, our progressive expectation is an invisible force, which drives the market.

Expectation can be presented in another way also. The economic definition of expectation is: "What people or businesses anticipate, especially in terms of markets and prices. Expectations are one of the five demand determinants and one of the five supply determinants. Changes in expectations then cause shifts in demand and supply curves, when they change". [2] Expectations are a set of assumptions, which people make about what will occur in the future. These assumptions guide individual investors, businesses and governments through their decision-making processes. Study of expectations is central to the study of market because it influences almost every aspect of the stock market.

Though expectations play a very important role in market analysis, estimation of what people assume about the future, especially when they make decisions in stock market, is really complicated. Before 1960, expectations were formed by the economists on the basis of past experience. This is termed as adaptive expectations.

Later on, John Muth in 1960s, developed a theory known as the Rational Expectations Theory (RET). According to the Rational Expectation Theory, expectations are based on observations and past experiences. It also states that the current expectations strongly influence the future performance. The RET assumption claims that people make economic decisions in a way that tend to take into account all available information bearing significantly on the future consequences of their decisions and they tend to use that information in a way so as not to repeat their past mistakes.

But some economists like Richard Shiller do not agree with the rational expectations about future. Accordingly, people are likely to form irrational opinions about the future events. The housing crisis or the sub-prime crisis that happened in 2008 is an example of irrational expectations.

2.3 Animal Sprit and Stock Market

An understanding of investor's behaviour in the securities market is important for the investors, companies and the government as well. Traditional economic theory assumes that every investor is a rational investor. In simple words, it means investors' decisions mainly depend on market fundamentals. Generally, rational behaviour refers to a decision-making process that is based on making choices that result in the optimal level of benefit for an individual, whereas irrational behaviour refers to when people make choices and decisions that go against the assumption of rational utility-maximising behaviour.

The Behavioural Finance Theory assumed that investors often behave irrationally when making their investment decisions so that there is incorrect pricing of securities, which causes market inefficiencies. Like individual irrational behaviour, sometime stock market also behaves irrationally to economic news; that news is likely to have no real effect on the fundamental value of a stock. Yet, this market behaviour may be more apparent than real. It is because of peoples' anticipations. The stock market may overreact in both the directions viz. up and down, by the press releases, rumours, excitement and mass panic behaviour.

The term *animal sprit* was used by well-known economist J.M. Keynes in his book titled *General Theory of Employment, Interest and Money*. The animal sprit describes the human emotion that drives consumers' confidence in the market. He argued that people might be irrationally guided in pursuing their economic self-interests and the only way people can make decisions in such an uncertain environment is, if they are guided by an animal spirit. In short, animal spirit describes the psychological factors that drive investors to take action, when faced with high volatility in the stock market.

According to the theory behind animal spirit, the decisions of business leaders are based on intuition and the behaviour of competitors rather than the analysis. Intuition in behavioural economics follows the laws of social psychology, which affect capital markets. It is found that the stock market is ruled psychologically, by either fear or greed. Fear is to lose money during the bear phase of the stock market cycle, whereas greed is investors' anticipation during the bull phase of the stock market cycle to make profit.

Recently, a well-known economist George A. Akerlof and Robert J. Shiller in their book titled, *Animal Spirits: How Human Psychology Drives the Economy and Why It Matters for Global Capitalism* explained about irrational emotional and psychological factors that affect economic decisions.

2.4 Behavioural Finance

Behavioural finance or *psychology of investing* is a subfield of behavioural economics. Richard Thaler is the founding father of behavioural finance. Though the study of behavioural finance in different literature became popular from 1990 but its references can found in 18th and early19th century literature also. A few examples include, MacKay's (1841) work *Extraordinary Popular Delusions and the Madness of Crowds;* LeBon's important work *The Crowd: A Study of the Popular Mind,* and Selden's (1912) book *Psychology of the Stock Market.* These were one of the first to apply the field of psychology directly into the stock market. In short, the above-mentioned literary works did show that emotional, psychological forces and group behaviour (crowd psychology) affect decisions of investors and traders in the financial markets.

Traditional theories believe in a 'rational man' and rationality of market participants feed into one of the classic theories of standard finance—the efficient market hypothesis (EMH). However, the beginning of this psychology-based finance (behavioural finance) research coincided with the start of many empirical findings that raised doubt on fundamentals of standard finance theory such as EMH and capital asset pricing model (CAPM). It assumes that people behave rationally and predictably.

Investor's behaviour may be affected by several factors. It can be divided into two parts, viz. internal and external factors. Internal factors are related to human psychology, sentiments and emotions which exist in the mind of investors. External factors include social or surrounding environment of which investors are a part and with which he or she interacts. This is nothing but 'social interaction' which decides investor's behaviour also.

"Sentiment describes a group of people's opinions, emotions or views, and market sentiment sums up such expectations for the market as a whole" (Thorp, 2004). Market sentiments are the feeling or general tone of a market, also called as crowd psychology. Market sentiments are revealed through the price movement of stocks traded in the securities market. In short, investor sentiment is an approach to measure the market sentiment. Behavioural finance examines the impact of investor sentiment on the stock market.

2.5 Other Theories

2.5.1 Prospect Theory: It is known as the loss-aversion theory. This theory was developed by psychologist Daniel Kahneman and Amos Tversky in 1979. It states that people's perceptions of gain and loss are skewed. That is, people are more afraid of a loss than they are stimulated by a gain. If people are given a choice of two different options, they will choice the one that carries less chance of a loss, rather than the one that offers the most gains.

Prospect theory deals with the idea that people do not always behave rationally. Accordingly, people look at the choices in terms of potential gains or losses in relation to a specific reference point. This is often a purchase price.

2.5.2 Regret Theory: It deals with how emotional reactions lead to errors of judgement. Generally, people (investors) follow the crowd and postpone to selling the stocks that has gone down in price (value), to avoid the regret of having made a bad investment choice.

2.5.3 Anchoring: It is also called as anchoring bias. It is a situation in which there is absence of better information. In such a situation, investors believe that current prices are right. Due to absence of any information, investors take reference of the past prices to determine today's price. Therefore, anchor is the most recently remembered price.

2.5.4 Over and Under Reaction: Overconfidence is a psychological bias in which investors overestimate their accuracy that a certain outcome will occur in the near future. The overconfidence bias affects the financial decisions of people in the stock market. There are so many examples where the market has *fooled* many sophisticated professionals and investors with high self-honour.

Generally, it is also found that people are likely to become more optimistic when stock prices go up and more pessimistic when market goes down.

To sum up, stock market reflects the collective independent decisions of millions of people. It is the way investors think and feel, affecting the way they behave when making investment decisions. These impacts are known as psychological biases. They affect all investors and vary depending on the type of investors. According to Richard Shiller, herding behaviour plays a decisive role in the human decision-making process. In the stock market, it is also observed that people are more optimistic than realistic.

2.5.5 Theory of Demand and Supply: It is a very classical theory or approach. According to it, the price of any stock is determined by the interplay of demand for a stock and the supply of the same (share). The price of a stock is not affected as much by a company's performance or the general political climate than by the interaction of supply and demand. Though this approach has been criticised on different grounds, it is clear that demand and supply forces play an important role in determining the prices of securities in the stock market.

2.5.6 Rational Expectations Theory: Initially, it was developed by the economist John F. Muth in 1961. Nevertheless, it was popularized by Robert Lucas and T. Sargent in the 1970s. In short, this theory says that a person will invest or spend, according to what he or she rationally believes will happen in the future. Following are some of the important highlights of this theory:

1. Individuals make decisions based on the best available information in the stock market.
2. Investors learn from past trends.
3. People will be wrong sometimes, but on an average, they will be correct.

2.5.7 Emotional Theory: According to this theory, psychological factors affect securities prices and cause shifts in the entire stock market. Traditional stock market theories rely on the assumption that stock traders make decisions in a fully rational and objective manner. But Human Emotion theory (HUEMO) stated that the assumption of traditional theories is unreliable in the real world. Stock traders make decisions based on psychological factors, including emotions.

2.6 Allocation of Personal Savings

One of the most important personal economic decisions anyone has to make is his asset allocation. It is found that there is very less awareness about 'personal asset allocation' in our country. There are many investments or saving options available for investors such as stocks, bonds, mutual funds, insurance, etc. and almost every investment carries a variable proportion of risk and returns. Also, risk and returns are highly correlated. Now, one question frequently asked is what proportion of savings should be invested in equities and bonds? There are many rules of asset allocation. The most common rule followed in the investment world is *the rule of thumb* or *the 100 rule*. This Rule says that equity percentage in an investor's portfolio should be equal to 100 minus his/her age. In other words, investment in debts should be equal to his/her age. Suppose, if an investor's age is 40 years, then he/she should have 40 percent of his/her investments in debt and the remaining 60 percent (i.e. 100 – his/her age) should be in equity. But this rule does not take care of investor's income, risk appetite, risk tolerance capacity, time frame of investment and investment goals. The allocation of assets is based on the basic principle of economics, that is, 'diversification of risk'.

World famous scientist Albert Einstein opined that compound interest is the most powerful force in the universe. It is the eighth wonder of the world. One who understands it, earns it; one who doesn't, pays for it. In short, allocation of assets is an art that every investor should follow. Presently, investment advisors are extending counselling to their clients about allocation of savings in securities such as stocks, bonds, mutual funds, or exchange traded funds.

2.7 Why Invest in Stock Market?

Generally, people think that saving means investment and vice-versa. But there is a difference between 'saving' and 'investment'. Personal saving is the money spared by cutting down current personal consumption. Personal investment means deployment of personal savings. Personal saving is parked in risk free low return products to meet future exigencies or planned purchases, while long-term risk investment is made to earn substantial returns.

In both the concepts, one thing is common, that is, the personal choice of an individual as to how much money is to be saved and where to invest that money. It has two dimensions: short-term and long-term perspective. Normally, saving has a limited value and returns and is parked in safe places that allow access at any point of time, for example, bank saving deposits, certificates of deposits. Whereas, investments can be churned to get the maximum benefits. It carries risks and includes stocks, bonds, and mutual funds etc. Talking from the return point of view, savings give little interest as compared with returns from investments. In case of an investment, the investor can lose the principal amount as well.

Endnotes

1. RBI, *Handbook of Statistics on Indian Economy*, 2018, p. 5.
2. http://glossary.econguru.com/economic-term/expectations.

3

Stock Market in India: An Overview

Stock market of India has been attracting world attention in recent years. The economic reforms started in early 1990s made the Indian financial system more market-oriented, efficient and transparent. The IT revolution in the financial services has changed the entire face of Indian capital market. These technological changes have not only introduced screen-based trading but also opened equal access to investors in a geographically vast country like India. The introduction of new technology enabled product innovations like future and options in the stock market.

There are so many options available for investment for an individual with stock market investment being one of them. Deposits, chit funds, post office savings, provident fund, jewellery, insurance, real estate etc. have been the traditional modes of household investments. Investment in shares has also been a traditional mode of investment. People purchase shares of different companies, but their purpose is to invest in securities of different companies to earn dividend. In recent times, stock market and real estate have turned out to be the modes of investment which have beaten all other forms of investments, due to higher returns.

Presently, National Stock Exchange (NSE) is the tenth largest stock exchange in the world in terms of market capitalisation. The Indian securities market in India is more modern in terms of infrastructure and adoption of international trade practices. Though stock market provides impressive returns, yet stock market penetration is very less in our country. Over a period of time, Indian stock market is becoming more and more mature with semi-weak form of market efficiency.

3.1 Structure of Indian Capital Market

Financial system is divided into money market and capital market. The stock market is a part of the capital market.

Capital market is a market for long-term funds. The distinction between capital market and money market is not watertight. Broadly speaking, capital market focuses on financing of fixed investment (machinery and equipment) while money market provides working capital finance (raw material etc.). Stock market is a part of the capital market.

Capital market channelizes household savings towards the corporate sector and allocates funds to firms. In this process, it allows both firms and households to share risks associated with the business. Moreover, capital market enables the valuation of firms on an almost continuous basis and plays an important role in the governance of the corporate sector.

An efficient capital market is an important constituent of a sound financial system. In India, efforts have been made in recent years to set up an effective regulatory framework covering major participants in the capital market. Similarly, the technology of trading and settlements in the stock exchanges has been upgraded. Internet-based trading in securities has been permitted. Foreign institutional investors (FIIs) and pension funds were allowed to enter the Indian stock market from 1993 onwards. The market has undergone a major transformation in terms of its structure, products, practices, spread, institutional framework and other important aspects like transparency, integrity and efficiency since then. The size of the market has also grown manifold.

The capital market fosters economic growth in following ways:

1. It augments the quantum of savings and capital formation in the economy.
2. It allocates capital efficiently thereby raising the productivity of investment.
3. It enhances the efficiency of a financial system as diverse competitors vie with each other for financial resources.
4. It adds to the financial deepening of the economy by

enlarging the financial sector and promoting the use of innovative, sophisticated and cost-effective financial instruments, which ultimately reduce the cost of capital.

5. Well-functioning capital markets also impose discipline on firms to perform.
6. Equity and debt markets stress on the banking sector by diversifying credit risk across the economy.

Figure 3.1 shows the structure of Indian capital market.

Figure 3.1: Indian Capital Market

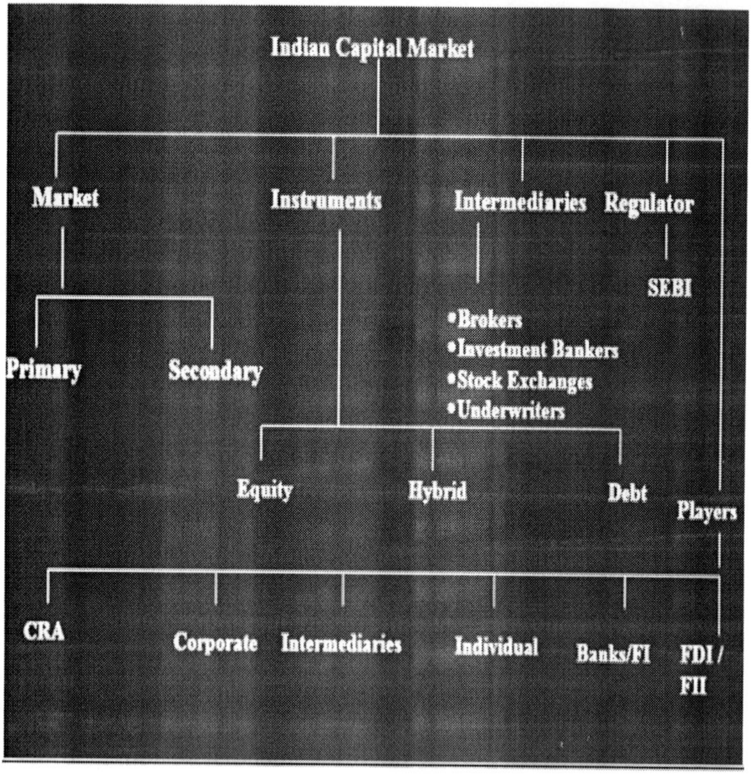

Capital market is a market where equity and debt market securities are traded. On the basis of nature of instruments, stock market is divided into primary and secondary market. Primary market provides platform for selling new securities to investors and raising direct capital for the company, while the secondary market is the market dealing in securities that are already issued by the company and listed on stock exchanges. Intermediaries in stock market are divided in two parts viz. primary market intermediaries and secondary market intermediaries.

Primary market intermediaries includes merchant bankers, underwriters, bankers to an issue, portfolio managers, debenture trustees, registrars to an issue and share transfer agents. Secondary market intermediaries include stock exchanges, brokers, sub-brokers, depositories (NSDL and CDSL, banks etc.). All these entities included in the eco-system of stock markets are regulated by the SEBI. It is an apex institution to regulate stock market. Players in stock market include CRA (central record keeping agency like NSDL), corporates, an individual, and financial institutions. After liberalisation of the economy, investment by FIIs (foreign institutional investors) and FDI (foreign direct investment) was allowed in the Indian economy which affects the stock market directly or indirectly.

3.2 Brief History of Indian Stock Market

During 1830s, trading in corporate securities and shares of bank and cotton presses took place in Bombay (Mumbai) city. Though the trading was broad but the number of brokers was hardly half a dozen during the period 1840 to 1850. Subsequently, a group of 20-22 stockbrokers initiated trading activities under a banyan tree which was opposite the Town Hall of Bombay city in the year 1860. This banyan tree still stands in the Horniman Circle Park, Mumbai. The stock exchange succeeded with about 60 stock brokers.

Actually, the ''Share Mania' in India started when the American Civil War (1861-65) broke out and as a result, cotton supply from United States to Europe was stopped. During this period, the number of brokers swelled to 250. The informal group of share brokers organised themselves as the Native Share and Stockbrokers Association (NSSA) which later in the year 1875, was formally organized as the Bombay Stock Exchange (BSE).

Therefore, the history of Indian stock market is rooted in the origin of Bombay Stock Exchange which is the oldest stock exchange not only in India but also in Asia. In the year 1899, the BSE moved into Brokers Hall and after the First World War, BSE was shifted to an old building near the Town Hall.

In the year 1928, the plot of land on which the BSE building currently stands at the intersection of Dalal Street, Bombay Samachar Marg and Hamam Street in Mumbai was acquired and a building was constructed in the year 1930. Thus, BSE started its functioning in 1939 till date at the same location.

Indian businessman Prem Chand Roychand (Cotton King of India) was a leading stockbroker and founder member of the BSE. He assisted in setting out traditions, rules and procedures for the trading of stocks at Bombay Stock Exchange.

Till 1992, our stock market was following the 'outcry system' which was replaced by BOLT (BSE Online Trading) system in 1995. The then finance minister, Dr. Manmohan Singh, presented his reform-oriented Union budget for the year 1991-92. It brought in a wave of privatisation, liberalisation and globalisation of the Indian economy. Besides this, the establishment of NSE and autonomy to SEBI followed by revolution in information and technology, has changed the entire face of the Indian stock market.

From the above accounts, it is clear that the history of Indian stock market is associated with the origin of Bombay Stock Exchange (BSE). Thus, BSE is not only the oldest stock in India but in Asia too. Stock market was basically spread over cities like Mumbai, Ahmedabad and Kolkata. Moreover, there was a significant participation of Gujarati and Marwarees in the Indian stock market. However, after the capital market reforms in India, situation has changed drastically. Now, due to the IT revolution, every village is connected to the stock market and everyone have equal access to it.

Historically, stock exchanges in India were started as a mutually governed self-regulated structure. Demutualisation of stock exchanges has been one of the significant landmarks in the history of stock exchanges in India.

3.3 Present Position of Indian Stock Market

The first stock exchange was set up in Mumbai in 1885. Since then, the number of stock exchanges in India grew to 23. Table 3.1 shows the expansion of stock market in India.

Though there are 22 stock exchanges but only two stock exchanges, viz. BSE and NSE are contributing to 99 percent of the total turnover (cash segment) of stock market in India. In this composition, the share of BSE is 5 percent while the share of NSE is 95 percent. Secondly, only 8 stock exchanges in the country have permanent recognition. Over the Counter Exchange of India (OTCEI) allows listing of small and medium sized companies. Among 22 stock exchanges, two are national level stock exchanges, namely Bombay Stock Exchange (BSE) and National Stock Exchange of India (NSE). The rest 20 are regional stock exchanges. Metropolitan Stock Exchange of India Ltd. was formerly known as MCX Stock Exchange. Hyderabad Stock Exchange, Coimbatore Stock Exchange and Saurashtra Kutch Stock Exchange were granted exit by SEBI on January 25, 2013, April 4, 2013 and April 5, 2013 respectively. Madhya Pradesh Stock Exchange was de-recognised in 2015.The OTCEI is no longer a functional exchange as it was de-recognised by SEBI vide its order dated March 31, 2015.

3.4 Refinements in Indian Stock Market

Indian stock market had a very long journey of more than 15 decades. It is now one of the emerging and most valued markets, playing a leading important role in the world stock market arena. It has passed through different stages of development. But looking at the last 25 years in particular, after the introduction of new economic policy, sea changes took place in the Indian capital market, which have changed the face of Indian stock market. Prior to the onset of economic reforms in 1991, the capital market structure in India was subject to several controls and was not transparent.

Table 3.1: Expansion of Stock Exchanges in India

S. No.	Name of the Exchange	Year of Establishment
1.	Ahmadabad Stock Exchange*	1894
2.	Bombay Stock Exchange*	1875
3.	Bangalore Stock Exchange*	1963
4.	Bhubaneswar Stock Exchange	1889
5.	Calcutta Stock Exchange*	1830
6.	Cochin Stock Exchange	1978
7.	Delhi Stock Exchange*	1947
8.	Gauhati Stock Exchange	1983
9.	Inter-Connected Stock Exchange of India	1998
10.	Jaipur Stock Exchange	1989
11.	Ludhiana Stock Exchange	1983
12.	MCX SX Exchange	2008
13.	Madhya Pradesh Stock Exchange*	1919
14.	Madras Stock Exchange*	1920
15.	Magadh Stock Exchange.	1986
16.	Mangalore Stock Exchange	1984
17.	National Stock Exchange of India*	1992
18.	OTC Exchange of India	1990
19.	Pune Stock Exchange	1982
20.	Vadodara Stock Exchange	1990
21.	U.P. Stock Exchange.	1982
22.	United Stock Exchange of India	2010

* indicates permanent recognition

Source: compiled from http://www.surfindia.com

Stock brokers assembled at the ring of the Bombay Stock

Exchange (BSE) on the trading floors called as *open outcry* trading system. It was carried out with paradoxical *badala* system (carry forward trade).The security market scam in June 1992 revealed inadequacy of and inefficiencies in the Indian financial system and prompted a drastic reform of the equity markets. Investors lost confidence and it made a paralyzing effect on the operation of stock exchanges.

The reforms initiated in the Indian capital market and with introduction of newer technology in trading activities, it changed the market practices and functioning of stock exchanges. The open outcry system was replaced by screen-based online trading system with nationwide access. SEBI Act was enacted in 1992, which gave it a statutory status. The Over the Counter Exchange of India (OTCEI) was set up in 1992 and National Stock Exchange (NSE) was set up in 1994. The National Securities Clearing Corporation (NSCC) and National Securities Depository Ltd. (NSDL) were set up in April 1995 and November 1996 respectively. These two institutions were set up for improved clearing and settlement and dematerialized trading.

The Securities Contracts (Regulation) Act, 1956 was amended in 1995-96 for the introduction of options trading with derivative products which resulted in a vibrant market for exchange-traded derivatives. Rolling settlement was also introduced in January 1998. It brought down the settlement system of stock exchange to a T+2 level. After two major scams, viz. the Harshad Mehta scam and Ketan Parekh scam, three major developments took place in the Indian stock market to avoid wild fluctuations. First, *badala* was discontinued in 2001, second, the introduction of circuit breaker, called the cut-off whenever index goes up by more than 10 percent, and third, SEBI Act was amended to make insider trading activities punishable as a serious offence. IPO scam in 2003-05 forced SEBI to make PAN (permanent account number) mandatory for all the applications. ASBA (Applications Supported by Blocked Amount) for all bidders was introduced in the year 2008.

To eliminate manipulation of stock prices, the concept of *market makers* was introduced. Accordingly, stock prices were determined by market forces such as demand and supply of shares. The entry of FIIs made Indian stock market more volatile. Now, even retail investors from abroad can invest in Indian securities market. Further, several mutual funds and insurance companies have invested through the institutional route. The merchant bankers have been permitted to take part in the securities market under the regulatory framework of SEBI. Mutual funds were promoted in capital market and linked with SIP, which mobilised investments of small investors in the stock market. Mutual fund is safe way to invest money in the stock market.

Online trading system in stock market has brought transparency in the market. Therefore, all the participants in stock market including brokers, regulators and public are able to know the prevailing price in the market at any point of time. Indian stock market is one of the best in the world in terms of technological upgradation. It has integrated with the global market. Introducing demat system in stock market has not only recorded every transaction in the stock market but also brought revenue for the government and restricted *benami* transactions. The stock market penetration in India is very low and therefore, SEBI, stock exchanges, mutual funds and merchant banks should give special attention towards educating the people about development of stock market and its investment opportunities.

Before capital market reforms, the most common techniques such as fundamental analysis, technical analysis and quantitative analysis were used to analyze the securities and their investment in the stock market, in a primitive and crude manner or not in a sophisticated manner. Now with the introduction of capital market reforms, stock market is more open and transparent for all the people. Professional fund managers have entered the stock market. These professional managers started using fundamental and technical analysis intensively and in a sophisticated manner. Basically, before reforms and after the reforms, while investing in securities, *hearsay* tradition was present in the stock market in the form of relatives, friends, brokers etc. Now, it also includes business news channels like CNBC, CNN-IBN, Money Control etc.

These days, given the advantages of technological interventions to smoothen the process of securities market transactions, Algoor High Frequency trading has become the buzzword in the stock market. In developed markets, like US, UK, and Singapore etc., the volume of such technology-driven transactions is significantly increasing over the years. Since 2008, Indian market is also gradually embracing the algo trading. The algorithmic trading is a technology platform providing an advantage of both the worlds –artificial intelligence and human intelligence.

3.5 Indian Stock Market in the Globalized Era

3.5.1 Foreign Capital in Indian Stock Market: Foreign capital is an important component of capital flows across the borders. It can be broadly divided into two parts: (a) FDI (creation of production facility), and (b) FPI (acquisition of securities). FDI is long-term global capital movement and FDI route is generally used by MNCs. FDI not only brings the capital to host country but also invites better managerial capabilities, governance practices, organisational skills and technology. On the other hand, FPI is a category of investment instrument that may be less permanent or short-term in nature. It does not represent any controlling stake in any enterprise but widens and deepens the stock market of a host country.

In India, FIIs cannot invest more 24 percent of the total paid up capital of a company. However, in certain companies which have passed a special resolution, FII can invest up to 49 percent. FIIs mostly invest in financial markets via equity instruments or bonds. FIIs can easily enter or exit the stock market as their basic purpose is to earn returns. FIIs are initially required to register with the SEBI.

FIIs can invest in all types of securities traded such as shares, debentures, warrants of listed or unlisted companies, government dated securities, commercial papers etc. in the primary market as well as the secondary market. FIIs can invest in unlisted companies also through the portfolio investment scheme (PIS). FIIs registered with SEBI can invest through equity market route and cent-percent debt route. The cent-percent debt route includes government securities, treasury bills, and non-convertible debentures of Indian companies. FIIs registered with SEBI can also purchase, hold and transfer Indian depository receipts of eligible companies which are resident outside India by following regulations outlined under FEMA.

3.5.2 ADR, GDR and IDR: Depository receipt (DR) is a mechanism through which a company of any country can raise finance from the international equity market. Generally, there are two depositories commonly used by Indian companies, viz., ADR (American Depository Receipt), and GDR (Global Depository Receipt). In this depository system, the shares of the company domiciled in one country are held by the depository i.e. overseas depository bank which issues claim against these shares. Such claims are known as depository receipts. Consequently, these receipts are listed on the stock exchanges. There are so many Indian companies listed on New York Stock Exchange (NYSE) under the American Depository Receipts (ADR) category. These include ICICI Bank Ltd., Infosys, HDFC Bank Ltd., Tata Steel etc.

A foreign company can access Indian securities market for raising funds through the issue of Indian Depository Receipts (IDRs). IDRs can be purchased by any person who is resident in India as defined under FEMA.

3.5.3 Integration of Stock Markets: Financial markets have become increasingly global. In case of India, this process began with the introduction of financial reforms programme since 1990s. Financial integration in the context of India's financial liberalization is significant because our country has become a crucial player in the world economy. Revolution in information technology (IT) has been playing a vital role in connecting financial activities across the countries. Along with various measures of economic reforms, opening up of home market to foreign investors was one of the significant steps taken by the Government, which lead to Indian stock markets getting significantly integrated with the stock markets of the world.

Due to globalisation, Indian stock market is also driven by developments in foreign stock markets of US, UK, Australia, France, Germany, Japan, China etc. There are so many studies based on co-integration models and Granger causality test have been conducted to study the integration of Indian stock market with other countries market from the short-run and long-run perspective. Most of studies concluded that developments in US stock market have important impact on stock markets at a global level including those of developed and developing countries like India, but not vice-versa.

It is generally believed that greater participation from global institutional investors also brings greater liquidity and improved reputation of the market, leading to better valuations for companies listed on Indian stock exchanges.

4

Basics of Primary Stock Market

4.1 Significance of Primary Market

There are two levels of security market: primary market and secondary market. Also called as the new issue market, primary market is an open platform for companies and government to raise long-term funds for business development. It is the first place where a company's securities are sold. A well-developed primary market is an indicator of capital market development.

Number of economic theories argued that economic development and growth happens in two ways: factor accumulations and productivity. Well-known economist Schumpeter opined that credit is the most important need of entrepreneurship and leads to innovations, product improvement and economic growth. There is lot of literature which provides empirical evidence in support of the role of financial institutions such as banks and stock market in general and primary market in particular in economic growth. Thus, primary market is an efficient vehicle for mobilisation of resources for economic development. Primary market facilitates companies to raise capital at a low cost. It provides method of diversification to reduce risk, as compared to the secondary market. Primary market restricts price manipulation and market fluctuations.

A well-developed primary market is necessary for the efficacy of economic policies of the government. There is a direct relationship between primary and secondary market. New issue market provides a direct link between prospective investors and the company. The health of the primary market depends on the secondary market and vice-versa. When the secondary market is in doldrums, the primary market is also discouraged.

4.2 Features of Primary Market

4.2.1 New Issue Market: The primary market or new issue market (NIM) raises new long-term capital. It is the market where the securities are sold to public for the first time, termed as initial public offer (IPO). Primary market is a platform whereby savings of individuals becomes the source of funds for the companies. It enables companies, financial institutions, governments and local authorities to obtain financial resources by issuing securities.

4.2.2 Precursor to Secondary Market: Though primary and secondary markets complement each other, primary market is the first step towards issuing of securities. Secondary market deals with those securities which are issued in the primary market and are listed on stock exchanges. Therefore, primary market is known as the new issue market while secondary market is known as the after-issue market.

4.2.3 Figurative Place: Secondary markets have a particular place such as stock exchanges while primary market does not entail any particular place. A primary market is a figurative place where securities make their debut. In short, it is a market where securities are created and investors buy securities that were never traded before.

4.2.4 Long-term Capital: Primary market helps companies to acquire capital for a very long period. Primary markets are used by the companies for raising fresh capital from the general public for expansion of business. Primary markets help a company to create their goodwill in the market. Fulfilment of long-term capital needs of companies is one of the important features of primary market.

4.2.5 Direct Dealing with Investors: In a primary market, securities are issued by a he company directly to investors through an initial public offering. In other words, investors directly buy securities from the issuer. In primary market, there are no intermediaries like secondary market as companies offer shares to investors directly. Primary market facilitates stakes in a company's ownership directly for the investors.

4.2.6 Less Volatility: Primary market is a less volatile market compared to the secondary market. The domestic as well as global factors make secondary market a more volatile one. As far as primary markets are concerned, they are not affected much by a lot of factors since the companies issue initial public offering only once. In short, price of securities does not fluctuate in the primary market. This market is more active during the bull phase of stock market.

4.2.7 Regulated Market: Like secondary market, primary market is also regulated by the SEBI and other entities in capital market. In case of primary markets, legal and regulatory requirements are strict which ensures that only quality companies approach stock exchanges for the issue of shares to the public. The Indian primary market is regulated by the Securities Contracts (Regulation) Act, 1956, Government Securities Act, 2006, Government Securities Regulations, 2007, and the Companies Act, 2013.

4.3 Economic Functions of a Primary Market

4.3.1 Raising Capital for Business: Companies come to the primary market to raise money for several reasons such as business expansion and development, improving infrastructure, repaying debts and many more. Primary market enables companies, government, and other institutions to raise funds through the sale of equity and debt-related securities. A company can raise capital from the primary market through various methods such as public issues, offer for sale, private placement, rights issue, and tender method.

4.3.2 Mobilising Savings: Primary market is an important source for mobilisation of savings in an economy. In this market, funds are mobilised from commoners for investing in other channels. Thus, primary market facilitates monetary resources being put into investment options.

4.3.3 Government Can also Raise Capital: Primary market operations of the RBI are mainly driven by the objectives of debt management policy. The government directly issues securities to the public via the primary market to fund public works projects such as construction of roads, building of schools etc. Primary market instrument includes treasury bills and government dated securities.

4.3.4 Open Market Operations: The success of monetary policy depends upon a well-developed money market. Open market operations are an important tool of monetary policy that a central bank uses to smoothen liquidity conditions throughout the year and regulate money supply in the economy. Primary market facilitates open market operations to regulate liquidity in the economy.

4.3.5 Vehicle for Foreign Investment: FIIs are allowed to invest in India's primary and secondary capital markets only under the country's portfolio investment scheme. Through foreign investment, companies can raise investment when they do not have sufficient funds to undertake expansion and development operations. Thus, primary market provides a platform to companies to raise funds from abroad.

4.4 Organisational Functions of the Primary Market

Primary market provides a platform for investors and companies to raise capital at lower costs. The securities issued in primary market can be immediately sold in secondary market where the rate of liquidity is higher. It provides facility of diversification of investment which reduces the overall risk. The functions of primary market are broadly divided into three categories. These are:

1. **Organization of a New Issue:** It is the origin of new issue which includes investigation of the viability of the project, analysis and processing of new project proposal.
2. **Underwriting of a New Issue:** It is an agreement between the underwriter and the new issuer of securities. The underwriter promises to subscribe to a specific number of shares in the event of public not subscribing to new issue.
3. **Distribution of the New Issue:** It is one of the key steps in the distribution of a new issue. The company issues a

prospectus, which is an open invitation to the public to purchase the issue. It gives details of the company, issue and the underwriters.

4.5 Different Type of Issues in Primary Market

There are different ways to issue stocks in the primary market. It is divided into three categories: (a) public issues, (b) offer for sale, and (c) others.

4.5.1 Public Issues: When a company raises capital by selling shares, bonds and debentures to general public, it is called as a public issue. For this reason, a company issues a prospectus which is called an offer document, which is again divided into two parts:

A. Initial Public Offer (IPO): When an unlisted company makes a public issue for first time, it is called as initial public offer. The shares of the unlisted company subsequently get listed on the stock exchange.

B. Further Public Offer (FPO): It means an already listed company makes another public issue to raise more funds.

4.5.2 Offer for Sale: Some institutions like venture funds or private equity funds invest in an unlisted company at an early stage of a company. When this company grows with time and when it becomes large, investors like venture funds, sell their shares to the public and the company gets listed on stock exchanges. The money of this issue goes to the existing investors and not the company.

4.5.3 Others: These are as under:

A. Rights Issue (RI): An existing company issues more shares to investors. In this case, the first invite goes to the existing shareholders of that company. This is called a rights issue and the shareholder may accept this offer or assign a part/all of it, to another person. It is also called as the letter of offer. The existing shareholders are free to apply for new shares *in proportion* to the number of shares already held by them.

B. Bonus Issue: Bonus shares are generally issued when a company earns extra profit or have extra reserves and they want to convert the same into share capital. These stocks are issued in proportion to the number of shares held by the existing shareholders of a company. In a bonus issue of the ratio of 1:2, the existing investor receives two new shares of the company for each share held. For example, an investor has 100 shares of an ABC company and the same company declares a bonus issue in the ratio of 1:2. Now, after the bonus issue, for the investor the share count goes up to 300 (100 existing + 200 bonus shares) shares.

4.6 Investors in Primary Market

They are generally classified under three categories:

1. **Retail Individual Investors (RIIs):** Those whose investment value is not more than ` 2 lakh.
2. **Non-institutional Investors (NIIs):** These include buyers and employees of the company, NRIs, companies, trusts or corporate sector, and individual investors whose investment limit is more than ` 2 lakh.
3. **Qualified Institutional Buyers (QIBs):** When a company wants to expand further, it needs capital. The primary capital market is an important platform for raising capital. Once a company gets listed on the stock exchanges, there are several ways to raise additional capital. QIB is one of them. QIBs include, among others, the following:

- Public financial institutions.
- Scheduled commercial banks.
- Mutual funds.
- Foreign institutional investors.
- Multilateral/bilateral development financial institutions.
- Venture capital funds.
- Foreign venture capital investors.
- Insurance companies.
- Provident funds.
- Pension funds.

4.7 Pricing of Public Issues

It is a very significant step during the process of initiating public issue in the primary market. The pricing of public issues may be in the form of: (a) book building issue, or (b) fixed price issue.

4.7.1 Book Building Pricing: Book building is mainly a price and demand discovery mechanism. It is determined on the basis of investors' feedback which assures investor demand at a different price. The issuer company mentions the minimum and maximum price band at which it will sell its shares to investors. The offer document mentions only the price band instead of the price at which its shares are offered to the public. The list of the bid received from investors at various price bands is known as the 'book' and can be seen online for each investor category. On the basis of the total demand in the 'book', the cut off price is then decided by the merchant banker and the issuer company. The 'cut off price' is the price, at which the cumulative demand for shares, should equal or exceed the offer size.

The process of book building is shown in Figure 4.2.

Figure 4.2: Book Building Process

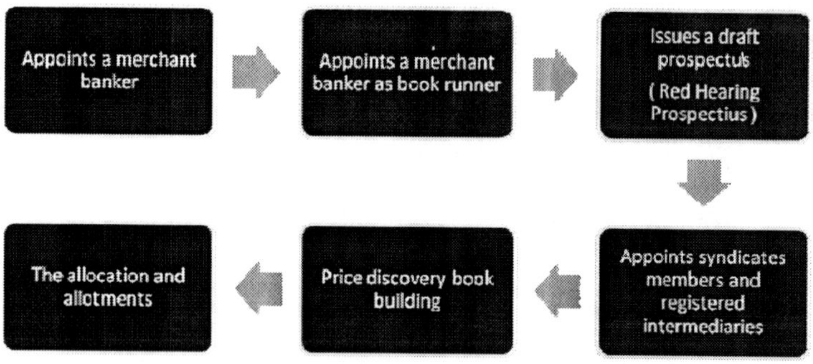

A. Appointment of Investment Banker: Investment bank has an important role in book building process. Therefore, the first step starts with appointing the lead investment banker. It performs the following tasks:

1. Propose the size of the capital issue.
2. Propose a price band for the shares to be sold.
3. Issue a prospectus with the price range.

B. Collecting Bids: Investors in the primary market are requested to bid to buy the shares of a company. Therefore, the investors are requested to bid the number of shares that they are willing to buy at various price bands.

C. Price Discovery: It is most important process of book building. After all the bids have been aggregated by the lead investment banker, they begin the process of price discovery based on bid analysis. The final price chosen is simply the weighted average of all the bids that have been received by the investment banker. This price is declared as the cut-off price.

D. Publicizing: It is the lead investment banker's duty to run advertisements containing the details of the bids received for the purchase of shares for a given period of time. Regulators like SEBI are also entitled to physically verify the bid applications if they wish to.

E. Allotment of Issue: All investors who applied for shares will be allotted shares at the cut-off price or issue price, proportionately.

4.7.2 Fixed Price Issue: The company decides the price at which it will sell its shares to the public and the same price will be mentioned in the offer document.

Investors can participate in primary market with PAN number, bank account and demat account details. Investors should read carefully the offer documents of public issucs which is available online on the SEBI website. The red herring prospectus is an important part of offer documents which contains all the relevant details except that of price or number of shares being offered. Thereafter, the application form along with ASBA facility will be available with stock brokers/ registrar to the issue (RTI) or bankers to the issue. The ASBA is an application or facility containing an authorization to block the application money in the bank account, for subscribing to an equity issue.

While investing in stock market, every investor should

know the difference between face value, market value and book value of shares.

4.8 Face Value of Shares

Face value is also called as the par value. It is the initial cost of the share fixed by a company. It is the base value of a share on which dividend is issued. Generally, face value is very less i.e. ` 10 which is determined on the basis of capital the company wishes to raise. Beside this, face value is also meant for accounting purposes to find out the equity share capital of the business.

Generally, face value has no relation to the market price. However, bond prices are influenced by their face value. Bonds are usually quoted as a percentage of the face value. Nevertheless, bond prices can increase (premium) or fall (discount) below their face value based on changes in interest rates and the financial health of the issuer company.

When stock prices climb above their face value, it is called premium and when it falls below their face value, it is called discount.

4.9 Market Value of Shares

Market value is determined by the interplay of demand and supply. It is the value at which the share is traded on the listed stock exchange. It represents a company's worth.

$$\text{Market value of shares} = \frac{\text{Total value of the company in the market}}{\text{Total number of shares issued by the company}}$$

In the context of primary market, we use two concepts frequently, namely: the bid price and the offer price. The bid price is the highest price a buyer of a stock is willing to pay. Whereas, the offer price is the lowest price a seller of a particular stock is willing to sell a share for.

4.10 Book Value of Shares

It means the value of the stock in a company's books. It

indicates the amount per share the shareholders can obtain if the company is liquidated and its assets are sold off to pay the liabilities. It is calculated by using following formula:

Book value per share =

$$\frac{\text{Total assets} - \text{total liabilities}}{\text{Total number of shares issued by the company}}$$

To recapitulate, the function of a stock market is two-fold: (a) to arrange for the raising of new capital (primary market function), and (b) to provide liquidity for existing securities (secondary market function). The new capital is raised through issue of shares and debentures. The corporate enterprises raising new capital may be new companies or existing companies planning expansion of their operations. Sometimes, existing private firms go public, i.e. become public limited companies.

5

Primary Stock Market in India

During the last two and half decades, there have been remarkable reforms in the Indian stock market. Consequently, new issue market (NIM) has made massive progress in recent years. SEBI is continuously ushering reforms regards the functioning of primary market. Our primary market has moved away from fixed-price offering to price discovery through screen-based auction for IPOs. This reflects a search to discover price through competitive auction. Now, price discovery in primary market is done in a fully transparent way, where all investors participate in an equal setting and the investment bankers' or other influencers cannot manipulate the allocation of shares.

5.1 Reforms in Indian Primary Market

Primary market in India has been going through the process of reforms for the last three decades. Before capital market reforms, the issue price in primary market was strictly determined on the basis of formula provided by CCI (Capital Issues (Control) Act, 1947. After the liberalization of Indian economy, the Controller of Capital Issues Act was abolished and the concept of free pricing of public issues was introduced. It was the beginning of a new phase in primary market in India. The issuing companies were made free to determine the issue price of their securities. To protect investors from heavy loss due to dubious companies, SEBI introduced the eligibility norms in the form of dividend track record of existing companies and compulsory appraisal of projects for new companies. It brought transparency in the primary market. It was seen that in the IPOs, that quality of disclosures in the offer documents was very poor. Important information was generally not disclosed in the offer document of a company.

Consequently, SEBI has introduced strict disclosure norms. In this respect, the Malegam Committee was appointed in 1995 to suggest measures to improve the quality of disclosure by Indian issuers. As part of the capital market reforms in general and primary market in particular, most of the recommendations of the Malegam Committee have been implemented.

In new issue market, the issue price was decided before the opening of the issue and therefore there was no clear idea about the market perception of price determination. The free-pricing method had a serious limitation in the mechanism. Therefore, SEBI introduced the book building mechanism to promote market driven pricing of securities. All the procedural formalities were streamlined. SEBI issued new guidelines to ensure a uniform procedure. Many aspects of the operations in new issue market were made more transparent. To control malpractices indulged by some of the intermediaries in the primary market, registration has been made mandatory for all the intermediaries including the merchant bankers and brokers etc. SEBI wants to bring professionalism in the functioning of intermediaries.

As a part of the investor protection policy, SEBI has made it compulsory for all the companies to disclose every bit of the information and risk factors regarding the projects undertaken by the concerned company. Also, the premium amount should also be disclosed by the company as per the SEBI norms. SEBI has advised the companies to follow the *code of ethics* for advertisement in media regarding the public issue. To reduce the cost of issue in primary market, SEBI has made underwriting of issue optional.

For efficient functioning of the primary market, the offer document is compulsory for a company. SEBI inspects the offer documents to make sure that the company listing the shares has made all the disclosures in it.

In order to make Indian capital markets more competitive and efficient, SEBI introduced QIB categorisation as an additional mode for listed companies to raise funds from domestic market in the form of qualified institutional placement (QIP). The concept of "anchor investors" has been introduced in public issues whereby 30 percent of the QIP portion will be allocated to anchor investors on a discretionary basis.

Introduction of demat mode in primary market is one of the significant steps which has ensured safer mode of subscribing to issues. As part of the reforms, private placement norms were also amended to simplify the processes, avoid duplication of disclosures, lessen regulatory interference and ensure greater self-regulation. As a part of IPO proceeds policy, SEBI plans to make it mandatory for all the companies to appoint a monitoring agency to keep a cap on use of capital raised through sale of shares, and to check any misuse of funds raised through IPOs.

In short, we can opine, that a major reform in the primary market has been improved disclosure standards. SEBI has introduced prudential norms and been promoting simplification of issue procedures. Companies are now required to disclose all material facts and specific risk factors associated with their projects while making public issues. SEBI has also introduced a code for advertisement for public issues for ensuring a fair and true picture. In order to reduce the cost of issue, the underwriting of issues has been made optional subject to the condition that the subscription is less than 90 percent of the amount offered. The book building process in the primary market has been introduced with a view to further strengthen the price fixing process. Besides this, preferential allotment rules have been amended rigorously.

The introduction of green shoe option and application supported by blocked amount (ASBA) by SEBI is a positive move in the capital market. The aim of green shoe option is to stabilize the post-listing share price of a stock. The aim of ASBA is to protect the money of investors and also make IPO issue process more efficient and less time consuming. As part of the reforms, now Indian companies have been allowed to raise funds from abroad through by issue of ADRs and GDRs.

5.2 IPO Grading and Credit Rating

As a part of SEBI Issue of Capital and Disclosure Requirements (ICDR) Regulations, IPO grading was first brought in as an optional feature in April 2006, but afterwards was made mandatory in May 2007. Again, it was made voluntary in 2013. The IPO grading is the grade assigned by a credit rating agency (CRAs) registered with SEBI, to the initial public offering of equity shares of a company. The grade indicates relative assessment of the fundamentals of that issue in relation to the other listed equity securities in India. It is helpful for investors to assess and compare fundamentals of a company. The grading pattern is depicted in Table 5.1.

Table 5.1: IPO Grading Pattern

S. No.	IPO Grade	Evaluation
1.	IPO grade 1	Poor fundamentals
2.	IPO grade 2	Below average fundamentals
3.	IPO grade 3	Average fundamentals
4.	IPO grade 4	Above average fundamentals
5.	IPO grade 5	Strong fundamentals

Source: SEBI.

While giving IPO grading, following points are generally taken into account by the grading agencies:

1. Company's business prospects and competitive position.
2. Financial strength and position of the company.
3. Company's management quality.
4. Compliance and litigation history of the company.
5. New projects, risks and prospects of the company.
6. Present corporate governance practices of the company.

Credit rating is called as IPO grading and red hearing prospectus includes the rating obtained by the issuing company from the credit rating agencies. Following are the top credit rating agencies in India:

1. CRISIL Ratings Ltd.
2. ICRA Ltd.
3. CARE Ratings Ltd.
4. Brickwork Ratings India Pvt. Ltd.
5. India Ratings and Research Private Ltd. (*formerly Fitch Ratings India Pvt. Ltd.*).
6. Acuite Ratings and Research Ltd.
7. Infomerics Valuation and Ratings Pvt. Ltd.

All the above credit rating agencies follow different grading scales.

5.3 Offer Documents in Primary Market

Offer document is a document which contains all the relevant information about a company. Offer document is called a 'prospectus' in case of a public issue and letter of offer in case of a rights issue. In India, along with low participation in stock market, it is observed that very less number of retail investors look at the prospectus issued by the company before applying for shares in an IPO market. This prospectus includes: draft of red herring prospectus (DRHP), red herring prospectus (RHP) or the final prospectus. As per Section 32 of the Companies Act, 2013, a company proposing to make an IPO should issue a red herring prospectus prior to the issue of prospectus.

5.3.1 Draft of Red Herring Prospectus (DRHP): It is also called as draft offer document. As per SEBI's guidelines regarding Issue of Capital and Disclosure Requirements Act, (ICDR Regulations), every company who wishes to list its stocks on stock exchanges must prepare a draft of red herring prospectus (draft offer documents).

The draft is prepared by the team of hired legal counsels including merchant bankers and underwriters. In the draft, it is expected that a company which wishes to list its stock, discloses clearly and honestly everything and anything which has happened or will happen in future.

Draft offer documents cover everything from the date of

incorporation of a company to the description of its core business and legal information.

The draft offer document is placed by SEBI on its website. It is also placed on the websites of recognized stock exchanges where specified securities are proposed to be listed and merchant bankers associated with the issue for public comments, for a period of at least 21 days.

5.3.2 Red Herring Prospectus (RHP): RHP is just like the horoscope of a company. It is a preliminary registration document that is filed with SEBI in the case of a book building issue. It does not have details of either price or number of shares being offered or the amount of issue. The main purpose of red herring prospectus is to attract potential investors by giving complete information such as performance of the company, future growth potential of the company, and senior management profile etc.

After filing of the RHP, company's management along with the merchant bankers arrange road shows etc. for marketing of the IPO and secure orders from the customers. Once bids are received and share price is fixed, the RHP is populated with the price figures and submitted again to the SEBI. Thus, the final prospectus includes: (i) price of the share, (ii) number of shares to be issued, and (iii) issue size,

5.4 Scams and Anomalies in Primary Market

To curb unethical practices in the stock market, a series of reforms have been initiated by SEBI, RBI and the government since early 1990s to streamline various segments of the securities market in India. Nonetheless, anomalies in the primary market still exist. Looking at the history of stock markets, everything is not fair in this market. There are so many examples of scams that have happened in the past including the Demat scam of 2005, the IPO scam of 2011, etc. These scams not only disturb the primary market but also hurt the sentiments of investors. Although there are no defined patterns of anomalies that exist, however, the following are some common malpractices.

5.4.1 Scam of Vanishing Companies: It means some companies do not follow listing rules and regulations and are not traceable physically on a given address. Over the last three decades, hundreds of companies have vanished after picking up crores of rupees from the investors. In spite of directions from various courts, none of the investors have received any compensation till date. These companies were found missing as they did not maintain their registers at the address as per the records with the Registrar of Companies or the stock exchanges. The Department of Company Affairs (DCA) has constituted 7 task forces region-wise to investigate the issue of vanishing companies. These task forces are coordinated by Coordinator and Monitoring Committee (CMC) set up by the Ministry of Finance, GoI.

With view to protect the interest of investors and to make the laws stricter against the vanishing companies, Section 205C was incorporated in the Companies Act, 1999. Also Section 274 of the Companies Act, 1956 was amended to make it more proactive regards the problem of vanishing companies.

5.4.2 Grey Market Activities: As academicians and new investors are always asking about grey market, therefore an attempt is made to address the functioning of grey market. Nowadays, grey market is working in case of almost all commodities. According to the business dictionary, grey market means goods or commodities are sold by non-authorized dealers at prices lower than the authorized dealers of that commodity. Talking about stock market, it is an unofficial market where an illegal agreement is entered into between an IPO investor and a stock broker allowing investors to lock profits before the stock lists. Under this system, shares allotted to IPO applicants are sold by brokers without transferring the shares to their accounts.

Following are characteristics of a grey stock market:

1. It is an unofficial market.

2. It sells stocks at prices lower than that of authorised dealers.
3. The grey market is a market that largely runs on trust.
4. It operates outside the purview of SEBI regulations.
5. All transactions in this market are in the form of forward transactions and open to counter party risks.
6. There are unofficial contracts represented by slips of paper.

5.4.3 Scams in the Primary Market: Stock market scams like the Harshad Mehta scam (1992) and the Ketan Parekh scam (2001) in capital market not only shook the Indian stock market but also caused a lot of financial distress for the common man.

IPO/DEMAT Scam 2003-06: It was about the misuse of shares allotment process in the primary market. During the period 2003 to 2005, shares of about 21 companies were allotted through IPOs. Some financers and market players manipulated IPO market by using *benami* (fictitious) demat accounts and subsequently the shares got transferred to the financiers on the first day of listing. A massive profit was earned because of the price difference between IPO price and the listing price. IPO scam came into light when Yes Bank launched its IPO in 2005. The prominent scammers included Roopalben Panchal, Purushottam Budhwani, and Himani Patel.

In the year 2005, Yes Bank launched its initial public offering and scammers like Roopalben Panchal manipulated the market by opening several fake demat accounts and then raised finances on the shares allotted to her through Bharat Overseas Bank, followed by Purushottam Budhwani who was controlling more than 5,000 illegal demat accounts. Another scammer Himani Patel opened 635 demat accounts and made 645 multiple applications. On the basis of the allotment, each application got about 16 stocks and the total numbers of shares amounted to 10,160. The surprising fact was that the shares with an IPO price of ` 510 were sold for ` 839 and the net earning grossed ` 33,52,636. Likewise, SEBI investigated scams in IPOs of some other companies also, including NTPC (National Thermal Power Corporation Limited), Jet Airways and Tata Consultancy Services (TCS). All these frauds had the same modus operandi of using fake demat accounts.

5.4.4 Price Rigging: It is a very common practice in stock market. It means price manipulation. Sometimes, companies artificially increase the price in the secondary market before a fresh issue in the primary market. This practice is generally indulged into by listed companies just before they make a rights issue or a fresh issue. Stock market scams like the Harshad Mehta scam, the Ketan Parekh scam or the Satyam scam etc. are the examples of price manipulations. Ketan Parekh and his associates were driving up share prices through creation of false or artificial volumes of listed stocks. In 1993, it happened with M.S. Shoes. In 1993, M.S. Shoes was trading at ` 25 and before its public issue, the price reached a high of about ` 500-600 in the stock market in 1995.

5.4.5 Insider Trading: It is also a type of stock market manipulation. It means the buying or selling of a stock by someone who has access to non-public information about a stock. There are two methods of insider trading: illegal or legal. It depends on when the insider makes the trade. It can be illegal when the material information is still non-public and trading is still executed which would be unfair to other investors who do not have access to such knowledge. It is an issue of information asymmetry, which is a cause for market failure.

In this regard, SEBI implemented the new insider trading regulations. Under such regulations, company insiders would have to disclose the details of all persons with whom they have significant financial relationships. As per SEBI's Prevention of Insider Trading (PIT) Regulations, boards of all the listed companies are expected to prepare a list of designated persons. These are the persons who have reasonable access to price sensitive information. The list could include promoters and board members of the company, and other key functionaries also.

6

Secondary Stock Market and Stock Exchanges in India

Secondary market is a market where securities are traded after the company has sold its shares in the primary market. The Bombay Stock Exchange (BSE) and National Stock Exchange of India Ltd. (NSE) are well-known secondary markets.

Indian stock market has been known to be world class in terms of trading architecture. It is well developed in terms of quantitative and qualitative perspectives. Quantitative parameters include amount raised from the market, the number of listed stocks, market capitalization, trading volume and turnover and other intermediaries. Qualitative parameters include establishment of nationwide screen-based trading system, dematerialization and electronic transfer of securities, rolling settlements, and sophisticated risk management.

In recent years, the Indian stock market has undergone sea changes. The economic reforms started since 1991 and a revolutionary change in information technology (IT) has changed the entire face of Indian stock market. In this chapter, an attempt has been made to study the functioning and development of secondary market in India.

6.1 Financial Markets in India

Financial market is a mechanism which allows people to buy and sell financial securities and other fungible items of value. Fungible means interchangeable or exchangeable items (like goods, services, currencies) in contrast to non-fungible items such as human beings. Thus, financial market can mean a capital market (trading in shares and bonds etc.), commodity market (trading in gold and silver etc.), foreign exchange market (trading in different currencies), and other such markets.

A well-functioning financial market enables efficient use of market-based instruments of monetary policy by improving interest rate signals in the economy. Apart from enhancing the efficiency of monetary policy, deep and well-functioning financial markets promote mobilisation of domestic savings and improve the allocative efficiency of financial intermediation, and foster necessary conditions to emerge as an international or a regional financial centre. Strong domestic financial markets also act as a buffer against external disturbances and help in absorbing shocks against the domestic banking system during crises.

Further, they provide incentives for development of hedging instruments, and lower macroeconomic volatility and financial instability. Efficient financial markets also have several indirect benefits such as rapid accumulation of physical and human capital, more stable investment financing, and faster technological progress.

Developed and well-integrated financial markets are critical for sustaining high growth, for the effective conduct of monetary policy, for developing a diversified financial system, financial integration and ensuring financial stability. The question therefore is not whether developed financial markets are needed, but how to go about in developing them fully. Financial markets presently deal with complex and sophisticated products. Introduction of such products would require clear regulatory frameworks, appropriate institutions and development of human resource skills. The speed for further changes in the financial markets would thus depend on how quickly are we able to meet these requirements.

The need for developed financial markets also arises in the context of increasing integration of domestic financial markets with international financial markets. The concept of globalisation is no longer restricted to its traditional sense—variety of cross-border transactions in goods and services—but also extends to international capital flows, driven by rapid and widespread diffusion of technology. In fact, most of the literature in recent years on globalisation has centred around financial integration due to the emergence of worldwide financial markets and the possibility of better access to external financing for a variety of domestic entities.

Financial market development is a complex and time-consuming process. There are no short cuts for developing well-functioning markets with depth and liquidity.

Some of the preconditions for financial market reforms are the following.

1. Macroeconomic stability.
2. Sound and efficient financial institutions and structure.
3. Prudential regulation and supervision.
4. Strong creditor rights.
5. Contract enforcement.

Structure of financial markets in India is shown in Figure 6.1.

6.2 Meaning and Features of Stock Exchange

The Indian Securities Contracts (Regulation) Act of 1956, defines stock exchange as, "an association, organization or body of individuals, whether incorporated or not, established for the purpose of assisting, regulating and controlling business in buying, selling and dealing in securities".

Features of stock exchange are as under:

1. Stock exchange is an organised market.
2. It is a market for company stocks and other financial securities.
3. It deals in second hand securities.
4. It ensures free and fair trade.
5. Allows dealings only in listed securities.
6. Transactions are effected only through members.
7. A stock exchange is an association of persons or body of individuals which may be registered.
8. Buying and selling of securities at the stock exchange are governed by the rules and regulations of stock exchange as well as SEBI guidelines.

Figure 6.1: Structure of Financial Markets in India

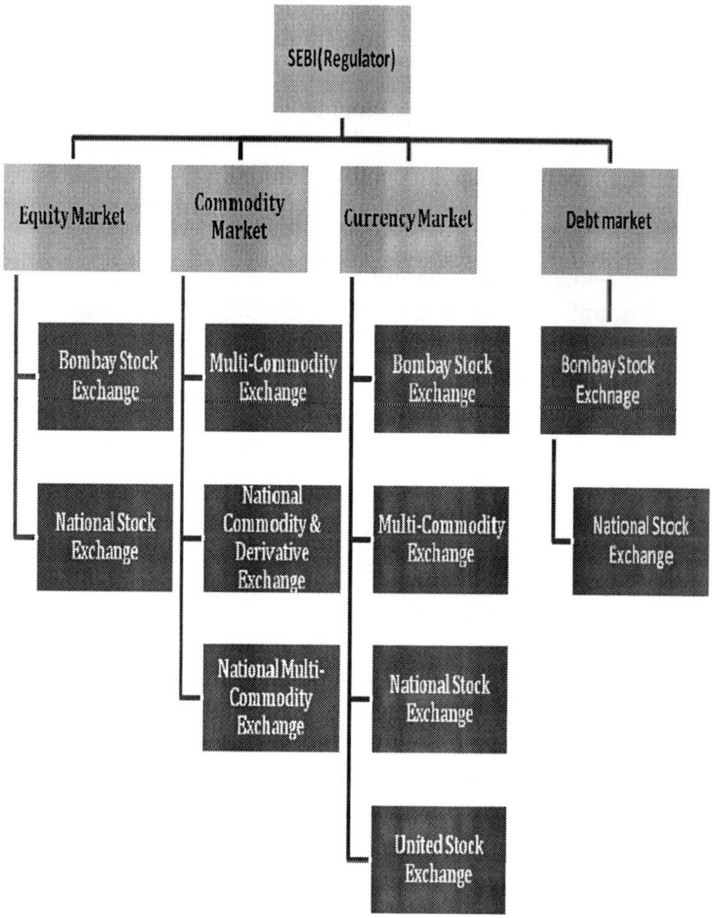

6.3 Economic Role of Stock Exchange

A stock exchange performs the following role:

1. **Stock Exchange Acts as the Main Intermediary**: A stock exchange is an institution which provides a platform for buying and selling of existing securities. It brings together prospective buyers and sellers; therefore stock

market is an intermediary between stock buyers and sellers.

2. **Facilitates Trading among Investors:** Investors find a proper platform, such as an organised stock exchange to liquidate the holdings. The securities that they hold can be sold to different buyers. At stock exchange, ownership of existing securities is exchanged between investors. In this process the company is not involved at all.
3. **Acts as a Barometer to the Economy:** A stock exchange serves as a barometer of a nation's economic and industrial health. It also broadcasts the ups, downs, trends and shifts of the domestic economy. It measures overall market and industry sentiment through a set of stocks that are representative of the market and the industry.
4. **Facilitates Price Discovery Process:** Stock market facilitates price discovery process which results from the interaction of buyers and sellers in the market. It acts as a medium of determining the price of stocks in a transaction consistent with demand and supply.
5. **Provision of Liquidity:** Stock exchanges ensure liquidity by providing a mechanism for investors to buy-sell securities. Whenever required, investors can convert their securities into cash. Thus, availability of a continuous market for sale and purchase of securities increases their marketability and enhances liquidity.
6. **Protects Investors:** Stock exchanges ensure that investing public gets a safe and fair deal in the market. It is an organised market and protects the interest of investors. Each stock exchange has its own laws and by-laws which every participant has to follow.
7. **Development of Primary Market:** The primary and secondary markets are complementary to each other. The efficient functioning of the stock exchanges creates a climate conductive for an active and growing primary market for new issues. Once the securities are issued in the primary market, they are then traded in the secondary market.

8. **Providing Scope for Speculation:** Speculation makes the market live and ensures liquidity and continuity in the stock market. Stock exchange provides sufficient scope for speculative activity but in a restricted and controlled manner.
9. **Spreads Equity Cult in the Country:** Stock exchange encourages people to invest in securities by providing security, investor's friendly trading practices and by educating public about the importance of investment in equity.

6.4 India's Premier Stock Exchanges

There are two premier national level stock exchanges in India, namely: Bombay Stock Exchange (BSE) and National Stock Exchange of India Ltd. (NSE).

6.4.1 Bombay Stock Exchange (BSE): The Bombay Stock Exchange (BSE) was set up in 1875 as 'The Native Share and Stock Brokers Association'. BSE is a stock exchange located on Dalal Street, Mumbai. It was the 8th largest stock exchange in the world by market capitalisation as in January 2022.

BSE is India's second oldest stock exchange (the oldest being the Calcutta Stock Exchange located at Lyons Range, Kolkata) and one of India's leading exchange groups.

In August 31, 1957, the BSE became the first stock exchange to be recognized by the Government of India under the Securities Contracts Regulation Act. In 1980, the exchange moved to the Phiroze Jeejeebhoy Towers at Dalal Street, Fort area. In 1986, it developed the BSE SENSEX index, giving the BSE a means to measure overall performance of the exchange. In 2000, the BSE used this index to open its derivatives market, trading futures contracts. The development of SENSEX options along with equity derivatives followed in 2001 and 2002, expanding the BSE's trading platform.

BSE has facilitated the growth of the Indian corporate sector by providing it an efficient capital-raising platform. BSE is a corporatized and demutualised entity, with a broad cardholder-base which includes two leading global exchanges, Deutsche Bourse, Fuse and Singapore Exchange as strategic partners. BSE provides an efficient and transparent market for trading in equity, debt instruments, derivatives, and mutual funds. It also has a platform for trading in equities of small-and-medium enterprises (SMEs). More than 5,200 companies are listed on BSE making it world's top most exchange in terms of listed members.

BSE also provides a host of other services to capital market participants including risk management, clearing, settlement, market data services and education. It has a global reach with customers around the world and a nationwide presence. BSE systems and processes are designed to safeguard market integrity, drive growth of the Indian capital market and stimulate innovation and competition across all market segments. BSE is the first exchange in India and second in the world to obtain an ISO 9001: 2000 certification. It is also the first exchange in the country and second in the world to receive Information Security Management System Standard BS 7799-2-2002 certification for its on-line trading system (BOLT).

It also operates one of the most respected capital market educational institutes in the country (the BSE Institute Ltd.). BSE also provides depository services through its Central Depository Services Ltd. (CDSL) arm.

BSE's popular equity index—the S&P BSE SENSEX (formerly SENSEX)—is India's most widely tracked stock market benchmark index. It is traded internationally on the EUREX as well as leading exchanges of the BRICS nations (Brazil, Russia, China and South Africa). On February 19, 2013, BSE entered into Strategic Partnership with S&P DOW JONES INDICES, and the SENSEX was renamed as S&P BSE SENSEX.

Historically an open outcry floor trading exchange, BSE switched to an electronic trading system in 1995. This automated, screen-based trading platform is called BSE online trading (BOLT). The BSE has also introduced the world's first centralized exchange-based internet trading system, BSEWEBx.co.in to enable investors anywhere in the world to trade on the BSE platform.

6.4.2 National Stock Exchange (NSE) of India Ltd.: NSE was established in the mid-1990s as a demutualised electronic exchange, located in Mumbai. NSE provides a modern, fully automated screen-based trading system, with over two lakh trading terminals, through which investors in every nook and corner of India can trade. NSE has played a critical role in reforming the Indian securities market and in bringing unparalleled transparency, efficiency and market integrity.

Though a number of other exchanges exist, NSE and the Bombay Stock Exchange (BSE) are the two most significant stock exchanges in India, and contribute to a majority of share transactions. NSE's flagship index, the CNX NIFTY 50, is used extensively by investors in India and around the world to take exposure to the Indian equities market.

NSE was started by a clutch of leading Indian financial institutions. It offers trading, clearing and settlement services in equity, debt and equity derivatives. It is India's largest exchange globally, in cash market trades, currency trading and index options. NSE has a diversified shareholding. There are many domestic and global institutions and companies that have a stake in the exchange.

NSC was incorporated in 1992 and was recognised as a stock exchange in 1993, at a time when P.V. Narasimha Rao was the Prime Minister of India and Dr. Manmohan Singh was the Finance Minister. It was set up to bring in transparency in the markets. Promoted by leading financial institutions, essentially led by IDBI at the behest of the Government of India, it was incorporated in November 1992 as a tax-paying company. In April 1993, it was recognised as a stock exchange under the Securities Contracts (Regulation) Act, 1956. NSE commenced operations in the wholesale debt market (WDM) segment in June 1994. The capital market (equities) segment of the NSE commenced operations in November 1994, while operations in the derivatives segment commenced in June 2000.

NSE changed the way the Indian markets functioned, in the early 1990s, by replacing floor-based trading with nationwide screen-based electronic trading, which took trading to the doorstep of investors. The exchange was mainly set up to bring in transparency in the markets.

Instead of trading membership being confined to a group of brokers, the NSE ensured that anyone who was qualified, experienced and met minimum financial requirements was allowed to trade.

In this context, the NSE was ahead of its times, when it separated ownership and management in the exchange under SEBI's supervision. The price information which could earlier be accessed only by a handful of people could now be seen by a client in a remote location with the same ease.

The paper-based settlement has been replaced by electronic depository-based accounts and settlement of trades. A robust risk management system is in place, so that settlement guarantees could protect investors against broker defaults.

NSE was also instrumental in creating the National Securities Depository Limited (NSDL) which allows investors to securely hold and transfer their shares and bonds electronically. It also allows investors to hold and trade in as few as one share or bond. This not only makes holding financial instruments convenient, but more importantly eliminates the need for paper certificates and greatly reduces the incidents of forged or fake certificates and fraudulent transactions that had plagued the Indian stock market. NSDL's security, combined with transparency, lower transaction prices and efficiency that the NSE offers, has greatly increased the attractiveness of the Indian stock market for domestic and international investors.

Currently, NSE has the following major segments of the capital market:

1. **Equities:** Equities, indices, mutual funds, exchange traded funds, initial public offerings, and security lending and

borrowing scheme.

2. **Derivatives:** Equity derivatives (including Global Indices like S&P 500, Dow Jones and FTSE), currency derivatives, and interest rate futures.
3. **Debt:** Corporate bonds.

A. Equity Derivatives: NSE commenced trading in derivatives with the launch of index futures on June 12, 2000. The futures and options segment of NSE has made a mark for itself globally. In the futures and options segment, trading in CNX Nifty Index, CNX IT Index, Bank Nifty Index, Nifty Midcap 50 index and single stock futures are available. Trading in Mini Nifty Futures and Options and Long-term Options on CNX Nifty are also available.

On August 29, 2011, NSE launched derivative contracts on the world's most followed equity indices, the S&P 500 and the Dow Jones Industrial Average. NSE is the first Indian exchange to launch global indices.

This is also the first time in the world that futures contracts on the S&P 500 index were introduced and listed on an exchange outside of their home country, US. The new contracts include futures on both the DJIA and the S&P 500, and options on the S&P 500.

On May 3, 2012, NSE launched derivative contracts (futures and options) on FTSE 100, the widely tracked index of the UK equity stock market. This was the first of its kind of an index of the UK equity stock market launched in India. FTSE 100 includes 100 largest UK listed blue chip companies.

On January 10, 2013, NSE signed a letter of intent with the Japan Exchange Group, Inc. (JPX) on preparing for the launch of CNX Nifty Index futures, a representative stock price index of India, on the Osaka Securities Exchange Co., Ltd. (OSE), a subsidiary of JPX.

Moving forward, both parties made preparations for the listing of yen-denominated CNX Nifty Index futures. Retail and institutional investors in Japan were able to take a view on the Indian markets in their own currency and in their own time zone. Investors therefore did not face any currency risk, because they would not have to invest in dollar denominated or rupee denominated contracts.

B. Currency Derivatives: In August 2008, currency derivatives were introduced in India by NSE with the launch of currency futures in US$ and INR. It also added currency futures in Euros, Pounds and Yen.

C. Interest Rate Futures: Interest rate futures were introduced for the first time in India by NSE on August 31, 2009, exactly one year after the launch of currency futures. NSE became the first stock exchange to get an approval for interest rate futures, as recommended by the SEBI-RBI committee.

D. Debt Market: On May 13, 2013, NSE launched India's first dedicated debt platform to provide a liquid and transparent trading platform for debt related products.

The debt segment provides an opportunity to retail investors to invest in corporate bonds on a liquid and transparent exchange platform. It also helps institutions who are holders of corporate bonds. It is an ideal platform to buy and sell at optimum prices and help corporates get adequate demand, when they are issuing the bonds.

Global ranking of Indian stock exchanges is shown in Table 6.1.

6.5 Stock Market Indices

Stock market indices are the barometers of the capital market. It not only mirrors the stock market behaviour but also the industrial development in a country. Stock market index gives an idea about the general price movement of the constituent companies that reflects the entire market.

The well-known stock market indices in India are SENSEX and NIFTY. Both SENSEX and NIFTY are scientifically designed and accepted worldwide as an indicator of Indian stock market (Table 6.2).

Table 6.1: Global Ranking of NSE and BSE

Stock Exchange	Country	Index	Rank as per Market Capitalization
New York Stock Exchange	USA	Dow Jones	1
NASDAQ	USA	NASDAQ Composite	2
Tokyo Stock Exchange	Japan	Nikkei 225	3
Shanghai Stock Exchange	China	Shanghai Composite	4
Hong Kong Stock Exchange	Hong Kong	Hang Seng	6
Bombay Stock Exchange	India	SENSEX	11
National Stock Exchange	India	Nifty 50	12

Source: Compiled from ISMR, 2020.

There are two methods of calculating stock market indices Sensex and NIFTY, namely: (a) price index and (b) total return index.

Price index takes into account stock price movements only. However, it does not consider the return from dividend payments of index constituent stocks. On the other hand, total return index reflects the returns on the index from stock prices fluctuation plus dividend payments by constituent index stocks.

Table 6.2: Prominent Stock Market Indices in India

Parameters	SENSEX	NIFTY 50
Stock Exchange	It is the flagship index of BSE Ltd.	It is the flagship index of NSE of India Ltd.
Date of Launch	January 1, 1985	April 1, 1996
Base Year	1978-79	1995
Base Index Value	100	1000
Calculation Method	From September 1, 2003, calculation method shifted to free- float market capitalization	From June 26, 2009, the computation was changed to free-float methodology
Number of Scrips	30 blue chip companies	50 blue chip companies
Index Calculated Frequency	The index is calculated real-time on all days that BSE Ltd. is open	The index is calculated real-time on all days that NSE of India Ltd. is open

The Sensex and NIFTY 50 are calculated by using the free-float market capitalization weighted method in which the level of the Index reflects the total market value of all the stocks in the Index as compared to the base period of Sensex and Nifty 50 (base year and its value is different for indices).

Market Capitalization	=	Shares outstanding* Price
Free Float Market Capitalization	=	Shares outstanding* Price * IWF (Investible weight factor
Index Value	=	$\frac{\text{Current Market Valuc}}{\text{Base Market Capital}}$ * Base Index Value

IWF as a term indicates a unit of floating shares expressed in terms of a number available for trading and which is not held by the entities having deliberate interest in a company. Generally, it is accepted that higher the IWF, greater is the number of shares held by investors as reported under public category.

Base market capital of the given Index is the aggregate

market capitalisation of each scrip in the Index during the base period. The market cap during the base period is equated to an Index value of 100 and 1000 for Sensex and Nifty 50, respectively.

6.6 Depository System

Introducing 'depository system' is one of the major landmarks in the history of stock market. Prior to dematerialisation, stock market trading and settlement was paper based, leading to increased cost and inefficiencies in the working of stock exchanges. It was time consuming also and proved difficult to find out bad deliveries. Therefore, lot of inconvenience was faced by the investors, brokers and regulators. However, the revolution in information technology has brought sea changes in the functioning of stock market. The depository system and dematerialisation of stocks are the products of development and application of information technology. Thus, the depository system replaced the rigid system of trade and settlement of stock market and introduced investor-friendly or user-friendly system.

The Depository Act, 1996 was passed to establish depositories in the share market with the objective of transferability of securities with speed, accuracy and security. There are three aspects of the depository system viz., dematerialisation of securities, freely transferable securities, and maintenance of ownership record.

Depository is an organisation which holds securities (shares, debentures, bonds, government securities, mutual fund units, ETF units) of investors in electronic form. It also provides service related to transactions in securities. There are two depositories working in India that is CDSL (Central Depository Security India Ltd.) and NSDL (National Securities Depository Ltd.). These two depositories are an example of duopoly market in India. The demat account which is compulsory for trading in Indian capital market cannot be opened directly with CDSL or NSDL but it can be opened only though DPs.

These depositories are functioning as per guidelines of:

1. The Depositories Act, 1996
2. SEBI (Depositories and Participant) Regulations.
3. CDSL and NSDL by-laws; and
4. Prevention of Money Laundering Act (PMLA), 2002.

6.6.1 National Securities Depository Ltd. (NSDL): NSDL is one of the largest depositories in the world. SEBI registered NSDL on June 7, 1996 as India's first depository to facilitate settlement of securities in a dematerialized form. It commenced its operations on November 6, 1996. It is promoted by Industrial Development Bank of India (IDBI), Unit Trust of India (UTI) and National Stock Exchange Limited (NSE). Subsequently, State Bank of India (SBI) also acquired a stake in NSDL.

6.6.2 Central Depository Security Ltd. (CDSL): CDSL is the second depository in India. SEBI granted it the commencement certificate on February 8, 1999 and it started operations on July 15, 1999. CSDL is an organisation promoted by Bombay Stock Exchange (BSE), in association with the Bank of India, Bank of Baroda, Housing Development Financial Corporation (HDFC) Bank and SBI.

6.6.3 Depository Participants (DPs): Depository operates through depository participants. The public sector, private sector and scheduled co-operative banks and big broking houses such as Motilal Oswal, Angel Broking, Asit C. Mehta, India Infoline Broking and Depository Services etc. are working as depository participants in Indian depository system.

6.7 Application of Circuit Breakers in Stock Market

Stock market is prone to fears and fluctuations. The victims/gainers of this situation are both companies (security issuers) and investors. Though the fluctuations (positive and negative) are an integral part of the stock market, sudden and huge fluctuations create threats for the reliability of financial markets. It may be due to price rigging or market manipulation. Therefore, SEBI has taken serious efforts to stop these malpractices by enforcing its by-laws and hence introduced circuit breaker for NSE-BSE indexes on June 28, 2001.

Basically, circuit breaker is an important part of daily trading on stock exchanges. Circuit means that a fluctuation threshold was set, keeping previous day close as the normal of this threshold. This threshold is set in both +ve and -ve directions of previous day close.

Circuit breaker means a halt in a particular equity trading. This halt may be for some hours or for whole day, based upon the intensity of breach. There may be an upper circuit breaker and a lower circuit breaker. All stocks do not have a circuit breaker. The equities which have derivatives do not have circuit breakers.

As per SEBI guidelines, "The index-based market-wide circuit breaker system applies at 3 stages of the index movement, either way viz. at 10%, 15% and 20%. These circuit breakers when triggered bring about a coordinated trading halt in all equity and equity derivative markets nationwide. The market-wide circuit breakers are triggered by movement of either the BSE Sensex or Nifty 50, whichever is breached earlier".

6.8 Debt Market Segment of Stock Exchange

Debt market plays a significant role in a growing economy which needs to provide a large and long-term amount of capital to industries for achieving the desired financial growth.

Capital market comprises of securities market and debt market. Debt market is a market for the issuance, trading and settlement in debt instruments of various types. It includes the securities which are issued by the Central and State Governments, banks, financial institutions, corporate bodies, statutory corporations or bodies etc.

Debt market instruments are traded on stock exchanges also. Both NSE and BSE debt market segments provide a platform for the development of a healthy, efficient and active WDM market mechanism and market structure in line with world class standards and greater integration with the global economy.

The Indian bond/debt market comprises of various types of bonds. The bond market can also be divided into two categories, namely, primary and secondary market. In the primary bond market, the general public or investment banks can purchase bonds.

6.8.1 Debt Market Segment of NSE and BSE: It is third most important segment of stock exchanges. In India, most of the corporate bonds are issued by private and public corporations which are traded in OTC (over the counter) market. The investors can buy and sell their bonds. There are different brokers who operate in the secondary market who facilitate these transactions.

The investors can trade (buy or sell) bonds just like equities, as these too are listed on the stock exchange. The investors can purchase G-secs with the help of an online service provider, such as Axis Direct, ICICI Direct etc. Even IDBI Bank has a G-sec portal where investors can easily buy and sell these bonds. But to do transitions, investors should have a demat account. In short, retail investors having a demat account can either buy and sell bonds by oneself on the stock exchanges or through brokers.

6.9 NSCCL and ICCL

The NSCCL (National Securities Clearing Corporation Limited), now called as NSE Clearing Limited, is a wholly owned subsidiary of NSE, whereas, ICCL (Indian Clearing Corporation Ltd.) is a subsidiary of BSE Ltd. NSCCL and ICCL perform functions of clearing, settlement, collateral management and risk management for various segments of NSE and BSE respectively. In short, both corporations act as the central counterparty to all the trades.

6.9.1 Objectives: These are as under:

1. To bring and sustain confidence in clearing and settlement of securities.
2. To promote and maintain, short and consistent settlement cycles.
3. To provide counter-party risk guarantee.
4. To operate a tight risk containment system.

ICCL settles all the trade reported on various segments of BSE, including equity cash, debt and equity derivatives including interest rate futures and currency derivatives. It also settles trade reported on BSE, SME, offer for sale, and securities lending and borrowing schemes (SLBS). Likewise, NSCCL settles trades in capital market, equity derivatives, currency derivatives, certificates of deposit, corporate bonds (reporting), commercial papers etc.

6.10 Derivative Market Segment of Stock Exchange

It is largest market segment of BSE and NSE. The Indian derivatives market has been in existence for a very long period, dating back to 1875. But after Independence, particularly in 1952, the Government of India officially laid a ban on cash settlement and options trading. This ban on commodities future trading was uplifted in the year 2000. The Security Contract Act was amended in December 1999 to include derivatives within the domain of securities. The *badla trading* on BSE was an example of future contracts. Through BSE, forward trading was there in the form of badla trading, but formally derivatives trading started its momentum in its present form after 2000 only. The NSE started trading in CNX Nifty index futures on June 2000, based on CNX Nifty 50 index.

In India, derivatives trading happen through NSE and BSE in equity segment. Similarly, in commodities, MCX and NCDEX (National Commodity and Derivatives Exchange) are their trading platforms. In case of trade in currency, it happens over NSE-SX and MCX-SX. Besides, derivative trade in bonds is also possible through the NSE platform.

A derivative is a contract between two or more parties. It is also a product whose value is based on an underlying financial asset (or set of assets). The underlying assets may be equity, forex, commodity or any other assets. Derivative is a risk management tool also.

Suppose, there is an XYZ share of a company and the current market price of share is ` 900, it would be called the underlying price and the lot size is 100. Assuming that the 30 days forward contract price is ` 910 (derived from underlying price). On expiry, the price may be greater than or less than ` 910. At the end of the forward contract, suppose it is at ` 850, it would then be treated as the actual market price. During the final settlement of forward contract, actual price will be compared with forward contract price of ` 910. In this example, the difference between actual market price (during settlement time) and forward contract price is of ` 60 (` 910-` 850) and total profit or loss is equal to 60*100= ` 6,000 which is either paid or received.

The word derivatives is used by traders to speculate on the future price movements of an underlying asset, without having to purchase the actual asset itself, in the hope of booking a profit.

Characteristics of a derivative market are:

1. Derivative contracts have fixed maturity and expire dates.
2. This market works in a lot size.
3. Derivatives can be used as leverage instruments.
4. They are traded on stock exchanges.
5. Its gains or loss depends on an underlying asset's value.
6. It has a low transaction cost.

6.10.1 Economic Functions of a Derivative Market:

1. To discover the price of future as well as current price.
2. Helps to transfer risk.
3. Speculative trade activities shift to a more controlled environment in a derivative market.
4. It helps to increase savings and investments in long-run.
5. It acts as a catalyst for new entrepreneur activity.

There are different types of derivatives such as commodity derivatives and financial derivatives like equity and forex. In recent years, the market for financial derivatives has grown tremendously in terms of turnover and variety of instruments.

6.10.2 Types/Structure of Derivatives: Generally, derivative market is divided into two parts viz., exchange traded derivatives and over the counter derivatives (OTC). Derivatives which are traded on stock exchanges are called as exchange trade derivatives while privately negotiated derivative contracts are called as OTC contracts. Recent advancements in IT have contributed significantly to the growth and expansion of derivatives market in India (Figure 6.2).

Figure 6.2: Derivatives Market in India

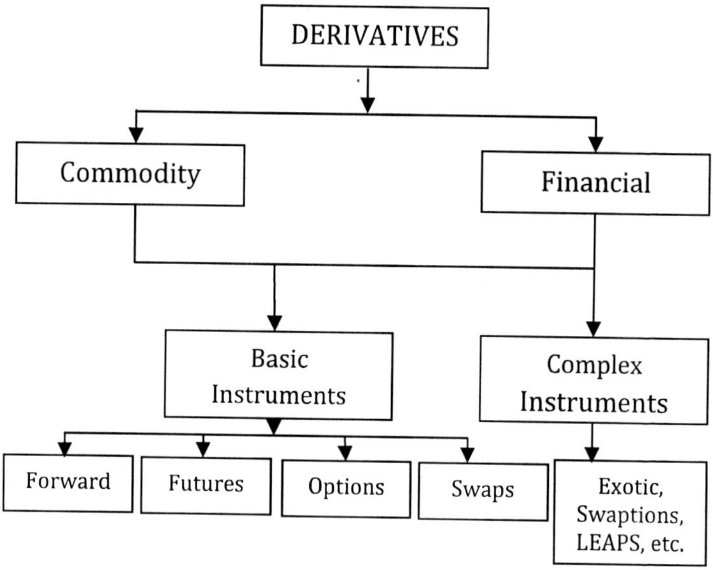

The derivative contracts or products have several alternatives. The most common variants (products) are: forward, futures, options, and swaps. Basically, these are equity derivatives instruments in India.

Forward: It is a customised contract between two individuals/parties, where settlement takes place on a specific future date at a pre-agreed price.

Futures: It is a special type of forward contract. A futures contract is an agreement between two individual or parties to buy or sell an asset at a certain time in the future at a certain price. Futures contracts are standardized exchange traded contracts.

Options: Options market makes up for a significant part of the Indian derivative market. An option is the right to buy or sell a security at a certain price within a specified time frame. The strategic use of options can allow you to mitigate risk in stock market. Normally, there are two types of options, viz. call and put option.

7

Stock Market Scams in India

This chapter outlines some of the major stock market scams that shook the entire nation and shattered investor's confidence in stock market. The three infamous stock market scams which took place include Harshad Mehta scam (1992), Ketan Parekh scam (2001), and the Satyam scam (2008). There were also a few other securities market scam including M.S. Shoes (1994), Sesa Goa (1995), C.R. Bhansali scam (1997), BPL, Videocon, and Sterlite (1998). However, the consequences of Harshad Mehta scam were so serious that the BSE remained closed for a month. The study of development of Indian stock market will remain incomplete without addressing the major scams. Here, an attempt is made to briefly review the three major scams in Indian stock market.

7.1 Harshad Mehta Scam

Harshad Mehta was known as the 'Big Bull' in Indian stock market. He was the founder of Grow More Research and Asset Management broking firm. In 1991, India was facing 'economic crisis' and the country embarked upon liberalisation by unleashing the 'New Economic Policy'.

During this period, as a part of monetary policy, every commercial bank by mandate had to maintain a fixed percentage in government fixed-income securities with the RBI, popularly known as the statutory liquidity ratio (SLR). Also, banks were not allowed to invest in stock markets. Their surplus capital was sitting in the bank vaults gathering dust. These banks then decided to loan their excess capital to banks who could not maintain the desired SLR in exchange for interest. Whenever banks needed funds, they used to sell their holdings of government securities to other banks and used it to avail loans for the short-term and after a few days the bank would have its government securities back after returning loan amount with an agreed interest rate.

In short, these transactions between banks were called ready forward deals (RFDs) and by using these deals, banks could secure short-term loan from other banks against collateral, i.e. government securities. In RFDs, brokers used to work as mediators. The role of these brokers was to find prospective buyers (banks) and sellers (banks) who wanted to buy and sell government securities. Here, being a broker, the role of Harshad Mehta as a mediator began. Harshad Mehta was a resourceful but an opportunist broker; he quickly found loopholes in the policy of RFDs and started using these loopholes for personal benefits.

Let us understand his money rolling policy with an example. Suppose there are four banks, i.e. bank A, B, C, and D and Harshad Mehta as a broker looks for buyers to sell the securities of bank A. He goes to bank B and takes money from them. In this transaction, Mehta asks both the banks for some time so as to get buyers and sellers. This way, Mehta kept the security of bank A, as well as money of bank B. According to RBI guidelines, no bank was supposed to issue a direct cheque in the name of any of the brokers. However, in this case, bank B issued cheque in the name of Harshad Mehta directly. The most surprising fact was that both banks A and B were unaware that in this transaction they were both directly dealing with Harshad Mehta.

It was because of his goodwill in the stock market, that banks trusted him; but he took advantage of this opportunity. He used this bank money received from B bank to manipulate stock market by raising stock prices. When Bank A asked him about securities, then he used to look for new banks seeking to buy government securities. Now, suppose if bank C is also looking for securities, Harshad Mehta went to bank C and would take money from them as he did previously with bank A and B and would again ask for some time to return the money.

In the meantime, he returned the money of bank A. In this way he would earn the trust of banks. Now to complete the deals of banks B and C, Harshad Mehta adopted the same policy. In this way, Harshad Mehta used RFDs as a chain system for rolling loads of bank money. He used this money to manipulate the stock market.

Now, one more important aspect of this scam was that when banks used to sell government securities to other banks for the short-term, the banks would give them a 'bank receipt' instead of the actual securities. Harshad Mehta took one more step in this scam when he needed more money to manipulate the stock market. He started issuing fake bank receipts with the help of some bank officials. The banks which wanted to buy government securities, Harshad Mehta used to give them fake receipts and banks used to issue cheque to him thinking that the given bank receipt is original. In this way, Mehta was earning loads of money illegally and was using it to manipulate some stocks by taking them to a higher level.

For example, he jacked up the stock price of ACC Company from ` 200 to ` 9,000. This way, Harshad Mehta pumped huge amount of money in the stock market and thus brought about a bull phase. As a result, common man also got attracted towards the stock market and invested their money into stocks. When stocks prices used to go up, Harshad Mehta use to sell his stocks at higher prices and return the bank fund and get back his fake receipt. This situation continued till stock prices were rising, but as nervous mood (bear phase) started in stock market, Harshad Mehta was facing losses and he was unable to return the bank money which he had raised against fake bank receipts.

During this period well-known journalist of ToI, Ms. Sucheta Dalal exposed the scam of Harshad Mehta. The banks came to know that they issued money to Harshad Mehta against fake bank receipts. Consequently, the banks suffered losses to the tune of ` 4,000 crore to ` 5,000 crore, and due to this, the stock market collapsed very badly and lots of investors lost their hard earned money. The chairman of Vijaya Bank committed suicide right after the scam was exposed.

Banks demanded their money back, but due to the bear run in stock market, Harshad Mehta was unable to return back their money. Finally, a lot of investors lost their money, banks lost their funds, and stock market crashed very badly. BSE remained closed for a month and later on CBI arrested Harshad Mehta by filing 600 action suits and 70 criminal cases against him.

7.2 Ketan Parekh Scam

After nine years of the Harshad Mehta scam in 2001, the second biggest scam to happen in Indian stock market was by a well-known chartered accountant named Ketan Parekh. This scam is known as the Ketan Parekh Scam. He was a bull in the stock market and used the policy of 'pump and dump' and 'circular trading' to artificially inflate prices of ten selected stocks, known as the K-10 stocks. It mostly consisted of companies from the information technology, communication and the entertainment sector.

His scam can be discussed in three parts.

7.2.1 Selection of Stocks: He preferred small companies, less volume stocks, future prospective stocks and stocks with lesser market capitalisation. Since 1997, the Dot.com boom had started in information, communication and entertainment sector and investors also preferred these IT-related sectors for investment. His preferred companies were Amitabh Bachchan Corporation, Zee, Pentafour, Tips, HFCL, Mukta Arts, Aftek, Infosys etc. These K-10 (Ketan-10) stocks continually increased, which attracted the retail investors towards them.

7.2.2 Sources of Fund for Ketan Parekh: It included his own capital, promoters' funds, institutional investors and banks. At that point of time, the RBI had allowed banks to give a maximum loan of ` 15 crore to companies. However, but by bribing bank officials, Ketan Parekh borrowed ` 800 crore from the MMCB (Madhavpura Mercantile Co-op Bank) and ` 100 crore from the GTB (Global Trust Bank) with collateral and sometimes without any collateral.

Ketan Parekh was using 'circular trading' strategy, with the help of his friends and some of the brokers (by giving commissions), and mutually bought and sold these stocks at the same time. This artificially increased volume and liquidity of the K-10 stocks. The main intention was to attract funds of institutional investors, including the mutual funds. During those days, K-10 stocks always remained in the top five positions.

7.2.3 Selection of Stock Exchange: Due to Harshad Mehta scam, lots of restrictions were imposed by the BSE. Therefore, Ketan Parekh selected the Calcutta Stock Exchange for his trading activities.

But once the 'Dot.com bubble' burst world-wide in 2001-2002, all the K-10 stocks witnessed a huge fall. Investors also started selling stocks and Calcutta Stock Exchange was in a payment crisis. Ketan Parekh was unable to sell the stocks or raise any new funds because the MMCB Bank and GTB Bank were close to being bankrupt.

Finally, Bank of India also a victim of this stock market scam, lodged a complaint against Ketan Parekh. In the end, lots of investors lost their money in stock market and around ` 40,000 crore vanished in this stock market scam.

7.3 Satyam Scam

The well- known Satyam Computers was a Hyderabad based IT Company. It was founded by Mr. Ramalinga Raju. It was the first Indian company to be listed on any international stock exchange like NYSE. Since 2001, real estate sector (property prices) was in boom. Ramalinga Raju was attracted toward this sector. Raju had inside information on the proposed Hyderabad metro route. He, therefore, incorporated Maytas Infrastructure and Maytas Properties and started buying land around the proposed metro route. This resulted in shortage of funds, and subsequently he started diverting funds of Satyam Computers to buy property. In order to get more funds, he started manipulating the books of accounts of his own Satyam Computers. In accounting term, it is called as policy of 'window dressing' whereby false and impressive financial results of Satyam Computers was released and the share prices of Satyam stocks started increasing impulsively. The rising prices of Satyam stocks increased their borrowing capacity with banks, as Raju was using stocks of Satyam as collateral against loans from banks. To meet the rising demand of money, he inflated the stock prices by raising fake sale invoices, and also manipulated bank statements to show higher cash reserves.

Ramalinga Raju and his promoters started selling their stake in Satyam Computers at rising prices and used the same money for investment in property. In 1992, at the time of listing with BSE, total stake of Satyam promoters was 24% which declined surprisingly to 2% in 2008. This scenario changed when the recession of 2008 hit Raju very hard as the prices of properties he bought declined sharply. Also, the gap between the real revenue and fake revenue of his company increased to such proportions that he had to reveal his fraud.

As a result, there was a big decrease in Satyam Computers price by 55% on NYSE in a single day. The immediate market reaction was the stock price of Satyam decreasing by ` 541 to ` 11.5 in 2009. Sensex dropped by 7.3%. Due to downfall in the market, the shareholders lost around ` 9,000 crore in a day.

In short, manipulation of books accounts was the main modus operandi. Though Satyam was already one of the fastest-growing IT companies in India, but his greed brought the empire to its knees and investors on street.

7.4 *Dabba* Trading in Indian Stock Market

In India, *dabba* trading (market box trading) is the proxy for stock market. It also called as *bucketing* in international market. Though SEBI has banned the practise of dabba trading, it is still operative in India. It is the process to trade out of the stock market. In short, dabba trading is an unauthorised market with its own trading laws and legislations. It is a process through which a broker routes the client to trade outside the stock exchange. Since it is an illegal activity, therefore, no income tax on profits or any commodities transaction tax (CTT) or securities transaction tax (STT) is incurred, which is a loss for government in terms of revenue. Also, in this market, there is no need of KYC and margin payment. The transactions of dabba trading are settled in cash every week which is off the record. It is an off the exchange trade, therefore, the participants have no right to redressal or complaints against anyone about it.

8

Fundamental Analysis of Stock Market

In stock market, investors put their hard-earned money into different stocks; therefore performing a research before making an investment is a must. It enables investors to identify the intrinsic worth of a security even before investing in it. Relying on stock investment tips and articles is not enough to give an assurance that investors will make a good buying and selling decision. Generally, to do the financial analysis in capital market there are two basic methods, namely fundamental analysis (FA) and technical analysis (TA). Both methods can help analysts and investors make informed decisions about investing. One common assumption behind FA and TA is that investment is a science as well as an art.

8.1 Fundamental Analysis

It is a method used by investors and analysts to identify intrinsic value of a stock. FA calculates financial ratios like efficiency, profitability, liquidity etc. to have clarity about the performance of a company. It is seen that the current price of a stock may not reflect the actual or true value of a stock. The stock may be overvalued or undervalued in the market. Therefore, fundamental analysis shows the economic health of a company in order to find out the intrinsic value of its stock. The main objective of fundamental analysis is to identify companies that are fundamentally sound or strong in order to invest in them for the long-term.

8.2 Features of Fundamental Analysis

1. It is based on economic and financial factors.
2. It follows a long-term approach.
3. It studies qualitative and quantitative factors that affect the

value of a stock.

4. It incorporates price sensitive information as and when available.
5. It uses financial reports like balance sheets, income statement, cash flow statement etc.
6. It considers information about earnings of company (i.e. quarterly earnings and projected future earnings).
7. It follows financial ratios like earnings per share, price to earnings ratio, return on equity etc.

8.3 Concept of Intrinsic Value of Shares

It is an anticipated or calculated value of a company's stock, which is determined through the fundamental analysis. It is generally considered as the present value of all future cash flows discounted at an appropriate rate. Internal factors like, a firm's products, its present management, and the strength of its brands in the market determines the intrinsic value. Generally, the most common valuation method used in finding a stock's fundamental value is the discounted cash flow (DCF) method. From the investors point of view it is said that:

- If real value of a share is more than the market price of a particular stock then **GO FOR IT...**means buy it.
- But if real value is less than the market price then **SAY GOOD BYE...**means not to buy.

Generally, fundamental analysis uses three sets of data:

1. **Historical Data**: It is used to know how things were earlier.
2. **Publicly Known Information about the Company:** It includes announcements made by the management.
3. **Unknown Public Information**: Information that is not known publicly but is useful, i.e. instances of how management handles crises, situations etc.

8.4 Components of Fundamental Analysis

The types of fundamental analysis are divided into two categories: qualitative and quantitative.

Qualitative fundamental analysis is based on the quality of parameters like, management, brand, products, financial performance, board etc. Qualitative analysis is a subjective opinion. The major source of quantitative data is extracted from the financial statements which is not subjective. In a nutshell, both qualitative and quantitative fundamental analyses of a company are a must to understand a company's health.

The process of fundamental analysis can also be done in two different ways viz. *top-down* and *bottom-up* fundamental analysis (Figure 8.1). The top-down approach starts with the consideration of overall health of the economy, industry and a specific company's performance. This approach takes into account various macroeconomic factors such as, interest rates, inflation, GDP levels, foreign investment etc. The bottom-up approach is primarily concentrated on various microeconomic factors such as company's earnings and financial metrics. In short, it is done by first looking at the individual companies and their internal assessment, followed by industry and economy.

Thus, fundamental analysis consists of three main parts:

1. Economic analysis.
2. Industry analysis.
3. Company analysis.

8.4.1 Economic Analysis: Stock market does not operate in a vacuum. It is an integral part of the whole economy of a country. There are coincidental indicators (co-movement of cyclicality), which highlight the current position of an economy. Some examples are:

1. **Procyclic**: Is one that moves in the same direction as the economy.
2. **Counter Cyclic**: Is the one that moves in the opposite direction as the economy.
3. **Acyclic:** Is the one that is not related to the health of the economy and generally of little use.

There are other factors also which have an impact upon the

economy.

Figure 8.1: Top-down and Bottom-up Fundamental Analysis

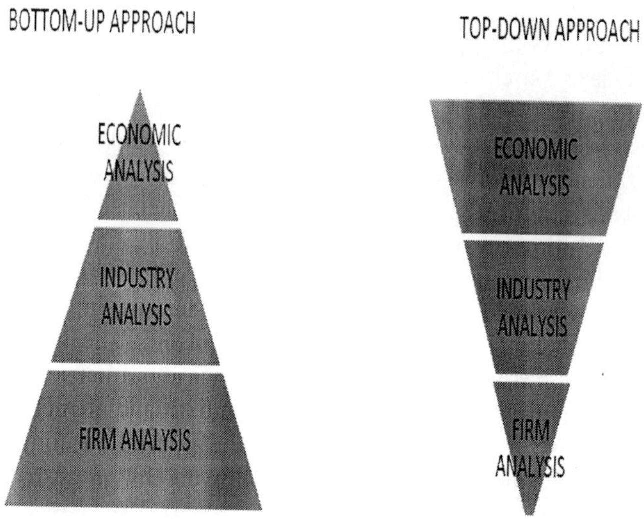

These are outlined below.

1. Gross domestic product
2. Inflation
3. Interest rates/monetary policy
4. Credit policies
5. Stock market
6. Foreign direct investment (FDI)
7. Foreign institutional investors (FIIs)
8. Tax policy/fiscal policy
9. Employment/unemployment
10. Political stability
11. Government policy

These factors impact economy in addition to the nature of working of a company. These macroeconomic factors affect economy in general and stock market in particular.

8.4.2 Industry Analysis: It is the second most important stage for fundamental analysis of a specific industry whereby its characteristics, past records, present state and future prospects are deliberated upon. It is very important to study these factors to decide the intrinsic value of a share.

Industry analysis is a capital market assessment tool used by analysts to understand the competitive dynamics of an industry. It helps them to get a sense of what is happening and what will happen in an industry.

Generally, it focuses on the following factors:

1. Demand-supply statistics of industry.
2. Degree of competition within the industry.
3. Future prospects of the industry.
4. Technological changes and its effect on industry.
5. Changes in credit system within the industry.
6. Influence of external factors on the industry.

Lifecycle of an industry passes through four phases as outlined below:

1. **Pioneer Stage:** First stage for a new industry with a period of 5 to 10 years being considered for this stage.
2. **Expansion Stage:** Enters expansion stage with new technology and business strategy.
3. **Stagnation Stage:** During this phase, things tend to slow down sometimes with an emphasis on increasing profit rather than achieving growth.
4. **Declining Stage:** This occurs when its products are no longer popular.

Other factors affecting the study of industry are:

1. Conditions of labour conditions within the industry.
2. Attitude of government towards the industry. Government policy with regards to a particular industry should be considered for the industry analysis.
3. Competitive conditions: It helps in analysis of the number of competitors in the industry and how easy or difficult it is for the new firms to enter the industry.
4. Past sale and earning performance: Historical performance of sales and earnings is studied on the basis of the past

behaviour; investors can then assess the relative magnitude of performance in future.
5. Stock prices of firms in the industry relative to their earnings.
6. Research and development activities.
7. Risk and returns promise expected by the industry.

8.4.3 Firm Analysis: Firm analysis evaluates a specific firm which seems promising in future. An attempt is made to identify future leaders in the upcoming sector/industry. After economic and industry analysis, this step helps us to narrow down and analyse the company at a microscopic level.

SWOT analysis is a very useful and popular tool for firm analysis. It examines the strengths, weaknesses, opportunities and threats pertaining to a company. SWOT analysis gives a qualitative impression about the company. For SWOT analysis, analysts collect information about company from the following sources, namely, prospectus, stock exchange, annual reports of the company, newspapers/magazine reports, research reports etc.

Firm analysis is a very broad subject. Generally, analysts follow certain major factors, outlined below.
1. Comparative advantages over its competitors.
2. Present market share and corporate image of a company.
3. Financial leverage and borrowing capacity of a company.
4. Firm's previous track record.
5. Financial stability and performance.
6. Operating efficiency.
7. Management of firm.
8. Future estimations of sales and profit.

8.5 Analysis of Financial Statements

It is an important part of company analysis. Financial statements include income statement, profit and loss statement, balance sheet, cash flows, etc. Most fundamental indicators about a company are reflected in the annual report of a company. Generally, following are the sections of an annual report of a company which are worth studying.

1. Financial highlights.
2. Management discussion and analysis.
3. Ten year financial highlights.
4. Director's report.
5. Report on corporate governance.
6. Notices.
7. Auditors report.
8. Annexures (if any).

8.5.1 Methods of Analysing Financial Statements: There are different methods of analysing financial statements of a company like, comparative statements, common size statements, trend ratios and ratio analysis. Ratio analysis is the most accepted and efficient method to analyse and compare financial statements of a company.

8.6 Limitations of Fundamental Analysis

1. **Availability of Authentic Data:** FA is based on available data about the company. However, if the management has incorrectly reported any financial details, there are possibilities of misinterpretation.
2. **Incorrect Assumption:** FA is based on assumed or projected growth rate, future interest rates and other factors. However, if these assumed projections go wrong, there is a possibility of incorrect interpretation.
3. **Over Reliance on Past Data:** This method uses historical financial data to predict future earnings, based on expected growth rate. Yet, historical data has its own limitations.
4. **Industrial Disruption:** If any unexpected changes happen in an economy such as introduction of higher tax rates, which would impact a company's profitability, there are possibilities of difficulty in interpretation.

To sum up, fundamental analysis examines companies' economic and financial reports, including all qualitative and quantitative information, in order to determine its intrinsic value. The main aim of fundamental analysis is to predict a company's future performance. To carry out a fundamental analysis, investors can follow either the 'top-down approach' or the 'bottom-up approach' or both. The top-down approach considers international and national economic indicators, such as, GDP growth rates, inflation and interest rates etc. and then narrows down to industry and the company. On the other hand, bottom-up approach is related to analysis within a specific sector irrespective of its industry or region. In short, fundamental analysis helps to find out good companies for investment but the valuation of stock through this method is based on financials provided by the company itself. It can be manipulated by the company to increase or decrease its share price. One needs to be aware of this window dressing and make an informed decision.

9

Technical Analysis of Stock Market

Technical analysis (TA) is an important tool of investment analysis. Presently, there is a growing trend among analysts to use TA as a tool to analyse stock market behaviour. FA guides about selection of stocks but it does not indicate about the right time to purchase that product whereas TA analysis guides about the right time to purchase and sell a stock. Technical analysts believe that past trading activity and price changes of a stock can be valuable indicators of a security's future price movements. The basic difference between FA and TA method is that the former focuses on a company's financials whereas the latter is based on historical price patterns or stock trends. Due to advanced technology and following the intensive use of computer facility, the TA method is very much popular and is widely accepted by researchers and analysts.

According to Martin Pring, "Price action in financial markets is a reflection of human nature, and human nature remains more or less constant. Technical principles can also be applied to any freely traded entity in any time frame". [1]

Technical analysis is defined as the art of identifying trend changes at an early stage and to maintain an investment or trading posture until the weight of the evidence indicates that the trend has reversed. [2]

9.1 History of Technical Analysis

The history of TA method dates back to 1800 in the works of Charles Dow. He is recognised as the father of modern day technical analysis. He developed a theory called The Dow Theory. This theory served as the basis for further development of technical analysis.

9.1.1 The Dow Theory: It is based on modern technical

analysis. Therefore, every academician and analyst should know the basics of Dow Theory.

Following are the basic principles of Dow Theory:

1. The price is a comprehensive reflection of all market forces.
2. Stock market has three movements, viz. main movement, medium swing and short swing.
3. A security's price reflects all the publicly available information. In short it discounts all the news.
4. Stock market trends have three phases: accumulation phase, public participation phase, and distribution phase.
5. Technical trends are confirmed by volume.
6. Past trading activity and price change of shares can be valuable indicators to understand a stock's future price movements.
7. There is a market sentiment behind stock price trends.
8. Price movements are not random.
9. *What* is more important than *Why*.

9.1.2 The Wave Theory: It is termed as the 'Elliott Wave theory', developed by Ralph Nelson Elliott. Now-a-days, this theory is employed by experts to analyse and forecast the future trends in stock market. This theory is based on the following assumptions:

1. The stock prices move in series of waves between optimism and pessimism for all market participants.
2. The 'psychology' of market stakeholders makes stock prices move in a certain pattern/trend.
3. Market moves in predefined patterns.

The central idea of this theory is that stock prices move in a series of waves. These waves can be broadly classified into three parts/trends that are:

1. Dominant trend (motive waves).
2. Corrective trend/waves.

A. Dominant Trend (Motive Waves): It consists of five waves. These five waves can be in either direction, upward or downward. There are sub-waves called as impulsive and corrective waves in the trend of five wave's direction. When the markets are rising, advancing waves are known as impulsive waves and declining waves are known as corrective waves. In falling markets, declining waves are known as impulsive waves and advancing waves are known as corrective waves.

B. Corrective Waves: It consists of three waves, namely A,B, and C, and these three waves of corrective trend start when the five wave dominant trend ends. The characteristics of these corrective waves are summarised in Table 9.1.

Table 9.1: Characteristics of Corrective Waves

Stage	Characteristics
A. Corrective wave	A small decline which gives the feeling that decline has again started. Volume in wave A is less than wave 5.
B. Impulsive wave	Wave B is the beginning of a new bull phase. Fundamental news is still positive and nobody is ready to accept the fact that markets can decline.
C. Corrective stage	The prices again start declining. Everyone realizes that market rally has ended. Market participation on sale side increases. The opposite happens when bears are in action and markets are declining. This includes 5 waves in down trend and three waves in up trend.

9.2 Tools and Techniques of Technical Analysis

The *indicators* are also called as *tools* of technical analysis. There are various types of indicators which measure the trend, momentum, volatility and many other aspects in the stock market. There are various types of techniques which are derived out of price, volume, time, and width data over time. Before we discuss various techniques of technical analysis, there is a need to understand the concept of 'trend' and 'trend line'.

Stock market movements happen in the form of trends. A trend is the general direction in which a security or market is headed. The trends are not always easy to see. In technical analysis, it is the series of highs and lows that constitute a trend. Basically, technical analysis is about the trend in stock prices. Well-known author Martin Pring defined it as: "A trend is a period in which a price moves in an irregular but persistent direction". [3]

Following are the types of trends:

1. **Up Trend:** A sequence of higher highs and higher lows.
2. **Down Trend**: A sequence of lower lows and lower highs.
3. **Reverse Trend:** A sequence which is broken.
4. **Sideways/Horizontal Trend:** A sequence which moves in a price range.

Trend line and channels are one of the most useful tools in the market. During an up trend, a trend line is formed by joining the lowest points of periodic pull-backs. To be more precise, we need two lows to join to form a trend line during an up move. During a down trend, a trend line is formed by joining the pull-back highs.

Channel lines are the addition of two parallel trend lines that act as strong areas of support and resistance.

"An upward trend line is said to be the area of support. The selling pressure meets the buying pressure here and eventually overtime when buying pressure is higher than selling pressure, price sees an upward bounce. A downward trend line is said to be the area of resistance. The selling pressure meets the buying pressure here and eventually overtime when selling pressure is higher than the buying pressure, price sees a decline". [4]

There are many tools or indicators of technical analysis. Professionals use these indicators on live charts.

Generally, these indicators/tools are divided into two parts:

1. **Breadth indicators**: Advance-decline line, McClellan Oscillator and McClellan Summation Index. These are

often used for technical analysis in intraday situations.

2. **Price based indicators:** Average directional index (ADX), commodity channel index, moving average convergence divergence (MACD), relative strength index (RSI), relative vigour index (RVI), stochastic oscillator, trixand vortex indicator.

Some of important indicators are discussed below.

9.3 Simple Moving Average (SMA)

The SMA is one of the most popular technical analysis tools used by traders and analysts in stock market. It is generally used to recognise trend direction, but can also be used to generate potential buy and sell signals in the stock market. It is calculated by adding the closing price of a security for the last n-periods and dividing it by the total number of time periods. SMA is formed by computing the average (mean) price of a security over a specified number of periods

$$SMA = \frac{CP1 + CP2 + CP3 \ldots\ldots CPn}{CPn}$$

Where,

SMA= Simple moving average

CP1, 2, 3....n: = Closing prices for the last n-periods

CPn = Total number of time periods.

- For short-term, SMA is for 5, 8, and 13 days.
- For medium-term, SMA is for 20, 34, and 50 days
- For long-term, SMA is for 100 and 200 days.

The 200 day SMA is a very popular method used by analysts in stock market. Oncc a moving average is calculated, it can be plotted on a chart of 200 days moving average price or 100 days, 50 days, 25 days, 10 days moving average line as per the choice.

However, one thing should be noted that shorter the time period of days, more sensitive it will be to price change and vice-versa.

It is also inferred that:

Stock price and moving average line	Signal of buy and sell
When stock price move above the moving average line	Buy signal
Stock price goes below the moving average line	Sell signal

9.4 Exponential Moving Average (EMA)

It is calculated by applying weight. This method gives more weightage, or importance, to recent price data in relation to older price. EMA can be calculated as a percent-based EMA or as a period-based EMA. To calculate EMA, there is need of EMA's weight multiplier.

$$\text{Weight Multiplier} = \frac{2}{(\text{selected time period} + 1)}$$

If select time is 10 days SMA, it is solved as follows:

$$\text{Weight Multiplier} = \frac{2}{(10 + 1)} = 18.18 \text{ percent}$$

The formula for an exponential moving average is:

EMA (current) = current price − previous EMA x multiplier + previous EMA.

9.5 Moving Average Convergence Divergence (MACD)

It is one of the most popular technical analysis tools. This indicator was developed by Gerald Appel in the late 1970s. It is a hybrid method of trend-leading indicator or trend-following indicator. This method is important to know whether a bullish or a bearish trend prevails in the market.

The MACD comprises of two lines:

- Fast moving average (fast MACD signal line), and
- Slow moving average (slow MACD signal line).

Methods to calculate MACD are shown in Table 9.2.

9.6 Relative Strength Index (RSI)

It is a momentum oscillator. It was developed by J. Welles

Wilder. It measures the speed and velocity of stock price movement of trading instruments over a specified period of time. RSI is a leading indicator and widely used by analysts.

Table 9.2: Methods to Calculate MACD

Step	Action	Line
1.	Select stock for analysis and the closing stock prices.	-
2.	Calculate 12 days EMA of the closing stock price.	-
3.	Calculate 26 days EMA of the closing stock price.	-
4.	Subtract the 26 days moving average from the 12 day moving average. (26 day EMA -12 day EMA).	Fast MACD line.
5.	Calculate 9 days EMA of the fast MACD line calculated above.	Slow MACD line.

The formula for calculating RSI is as follows:

$$RSI = \frac{100 - 100}{(1 + RS)}$$

RSI = Average gain over a specified period/Average loss over the same period.

RSI index is plotted in the range of 0-100 and it is considered that:

RSI Index	Zone	Buy/Sale Signal
Above 70	Stock is overbought	Can sell stock
30-70	Normal zone	------
Below 30	Stock is over sold	Can buy the stock

9.7 Average Directional Index (ADX)

It was developed by J. Welles Wilder in 1987. It is an

indicator of the strength of a stock's trend. This method is helpful in deciding whether the trend of a particular stock is strong or not. ADX quantifies the velocity of a stock price, regardless its movement.

In this method, positive directional indicator (+DI) and negative directional indicator (-DI) are used on the stock charting system which act as complements to ADX method. According to this method:

ADX Index Range	Market Trend
Above 25	Strong
Below 25	No trend

9.8 Stochastic Oscillator Indicator

It was invented by a renowned technical analyst George C. Lane in 1950. The Stochastic is one of the popular technical indicator or tools used by stock analysts. This indicator is easy to understand and has a high degree of accuracy. This indicator is used to show when a security has moved into an overbought or oversold position.

Formula of Stochastic Oscillator Indicator:

It is measured with two lines viz., the 'K' line (indicator line) and the 'D' line (signal or trigger line).

$$K = \frac{100 * (CP - L14)}{(H14 - L14)}$$

Where,

CP: The current closing price

L14: The lowest price of the 14 previous trading sessions

H14: The highest price of the same 14 previous trading sessions

$$D = 100(H3 \div L3)$$

Where,

H3: The highest of the three previous trading sessions

L3: The lowest price traded during the same three-day period.

- Stochastic indicator itself can range only from 0 to 100.
- A reading over 80 reflects overbought market conditions.
- A reading below 20 reflects oversold market conditions.

9.9 Aroon Indicator

It was developed by Tushar Chande in 1995. It is a tool that determines whether a stock is trending or not and how strong the trend is. This indicator uses magnitude of stock trend. The Aroon indicator is shown in percentage terms and fluctuates between 0 and 100. There are two separate indicators, namely, Aroon-up and Aroon-down. The formula to calculate these two is mentioned below:

$$Aroon - Up = \frac{(25 - Days\ Since\ 25 - day\ High)}{25} * 100$$

$$Aroon - down = \frac{(25 - Days\ Since\ 25 - day\ Low)}{25} * 100$$

If Aroon-up line is above 70, there is an upward trend in the selected stock. If Aroon-up line is below 70, there is a downward trend in the selected stock. This method is required to find out the high and low stock price for the last 25 days.

Aroon Value Range	Trend in Market
Close to 100	Stronger trend
Close to zero	Weaker

9.10 Fear Index

The VIX or volatility index is better known as the fear index—higher the fear in the market, higher the level of VIX. It is an important index in the world of trading and investment because it provides a quantifiable measure of market risk and investors' sentiments. Volatility can be measured by using two different methods. First method is a statistical method. It includes statistical numbers like mean (average), variance, and finally the standard deviation on a set of historical price data.

The resulting value of standard deviation is a measure of risk or volatility. The second method to measure volatility involves assuming its value, as implied by option prices. Options are derivative instruments whose price depends upon the probability of a particular stock's current price, moving enough to reach a particular level (called the strike price or the exercise price).

9.11 Bull and Bear Phases in Stock Market

Bull and bear are two animals that represent natural or general tendency of human behaviour or human psychology. Bullish and bearish phases are speculative phases in stock market, making it lively. A market price moving in trend is one of the major components of stock market technical analysis. Market trends are described as direction in which stock market is moving or sustaining movement over a period of time. The term bull market and bear market describe upward and downward movement respectively and these trends are quite natural in stock market. The expression bullish means optimistic and bearish indicates pessimism.

A bull market is a prolonged period in which investment and prices rise. A bull market tends to be associated with increasing investor confidence, thereby motivating investors to buy in anticipation, for future capital gains. Contrarily, a bear market is a prolonged period in which prices fall, accompanied by widespread pessimism. Investors anticipating further losses are motivated to sell, with negative sentiment feeding on itself in a vicious circle.

There are different methods to measure bull and bear phases in stock market; the popular one being the 'Day Moving Average' (DMA-200) or SMA-200 method. These have been used to calculate the bull and bear phases in stock market. The bulls are active above the DMA-200 and bears are active blow the DMA-200.

9.12 Trading Strategies

Major trading strategies used in stock market are shown in

Figure 9.1.

Figure 9.1: Major Trading Strategies

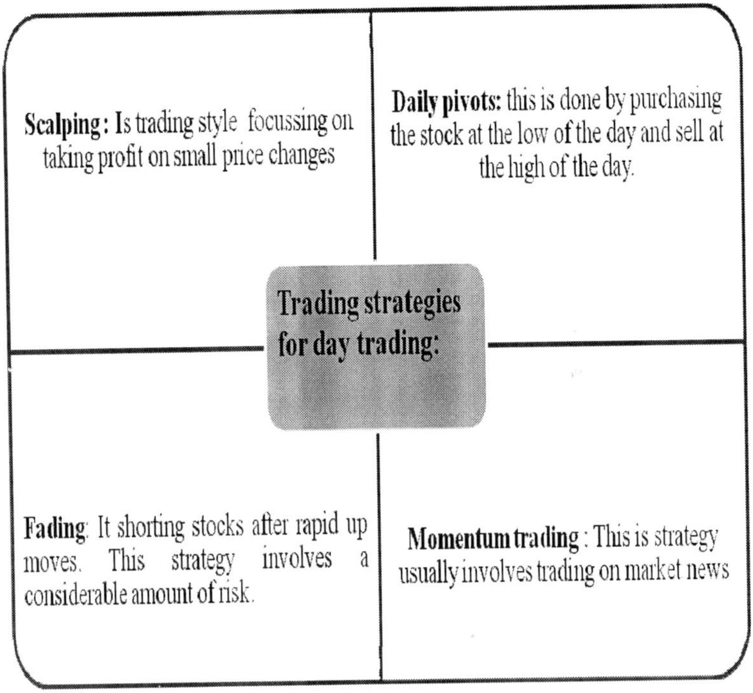

9.13 Application of Artificial Intelligence (AI) and Algorithm Trading (AT)

Artificial intelligence (AI) is a machine learning technique. It learns structure of the data and tries to forecast about future trends in stock market. AI is increasingly becoming a part of our lives. It is applied in all the fields of knowledge. AI has been a game changer for the stock market and is currently used extensively in algorithm trading.

Algorithm Trading (AT) is a system of trading which uses AI for decision-making in the financial markets by employing advanced mathematical tools and techniques. 'Algo trading' has a predefined set of processes, applied to buy and sell stocks accurately in a successful manner.

Algo trading can develop decisions based on market information which are received electronically and these decisions are performed automatically. Expansion of AT can shift stock market transactions from 'human' to 'machines'.

9.14 Major Limitations of Technical Analysis

1. TA is based on a theory. If the indicators give mixed signals, then there is possibility of indecision.
2. It is all about probability.
3. There is possibility of a biased view among the analysts.
4. The random walk hypothesis casts its shadow over the validity of technical analysis.
5. The forecasting accuracy is not 100%.

To sum up, FA helps in understanding the financial performance of a company, while TA helps in observing the patterns of share price movement of a company. Investors can use either or both fundamental and technical analysis to decide the entry and exit points while trading in stocks. The fundamental and technical analysis is based on past events, but the choice of which methods for analysis should be used is determined by the investor's belief in different paradigms for "how the stock market actually works.

Endnotes

1. Martin Pring (2014), "Technical Analysis Explained", fifth edition, McGraw Hill, New Delhi.
2. Ibid.
3. Ibid.
4. "A Handbook of Technical Analysis", available at: https://www.elearnmarkets.com/uploads/content_pdf/MxudjQevBU.pdf.

10

Measurement of Returns, Risks and Volatility in Stock Market

Returns, risks and volatility are an integral part of stock market and these three elements are associated with investment in stock market. Therefore, issues of risk, return and volatility have become increasingly important in recent times for all the stakeholders of stock market. In this chapter, an attempt is made to introduce the concept of returns, risk and volatility in stock market.

10.1 Measurement of Stock Returns

Investors in their investment decisions aim at returns, which they try to maximize subsequently. Returns from investing in equity comprises of dividends and capital gains. Returns are the motivating factor for investors. Returns means the profit earned as result of rise in share prices. [1] Returns help investors to compare the benefits available in the alternative investment avenue. Each investor would be holding securities in his portfolio in which the expected return is the highest.

In stock market, returns can be calculated for a particular stock and also returns regard the stock indices such as Sensex and NIFTY. Stock returns can be calculated daily, weekly, monthly or on a yearly basis.

Generally, rate of returns is calculated as follows: [2]

$$r_t = \frac{P_t - P_{t-1}}{P_{t-1}} * 100$$

Where,

r_t = the rate of return for the period t

P_t and P_{t-1} are the prices of the two successive periods, viz., t and t-1.

An alternative mode of calculating rate of return is the logarithmic difference of price of two successive periods. Symbolically,

$$r_t = \log_e\left(\frac{P_t}{P_{t-1}}\right) = \log_e(P_t) - \log_e(P_{t-1})$$

Where,

$\log_e$: is natural logarithm,

P_t and P_{t-1} are the prices for the two successive periods, viz., t and t-1.

r_t = market return at the period t.

The income source from a stock is dividends and its increase in value. Therefore, the rate of stock returns is calculated as follows:

$$r_t = \frac{(P_t - P_{t-1}) + D}{P_{t-1}} * 100$$

Where,

D= Dividends

10.2 Measurement of Risk

The growth of markets for financial assets created a need for risk measures. Risk can be studied from industry point of view or from investor's point of view. Risk measures the uncertainty that an investor is willing to take to realize a gain from an investment.

Generally, stock market is subject to two types of risks, namely, systematic (market risk) and unsystematic (non-market risk). Systematic risk is the risk that a particular stock's price will be affected by the overall stock market and economic movements.

Unsystematic risk is associated with a company's or its industry's weak economic position that will adversely affect the stock's price. In stock market, we have to take many decisions under the situations of risk and uncertainty. According to American economist Frank Knight, there is a difference between risk and uncertainty and its measurement. It is said about risk and uncertainty that 'risk is a measurable uncertainty while uncertainty is an immeasurable risk. The concept of risk is based on probability analysis.

Types of Risks: Generally, a financial market classifies risks into two parts:

1. Systematic risk, and
2. Unsystematic risk.

The systematic risk is a market level risk. It affects all businesses equally. On the other hand, unsystematic risk is specific to a company or a sector.

Measures of Risk: Important measures of risk in stock market are shown in Table 10.1.

10.3 The Concept of Volatility

Volatility is an effective measure to understand the market sentiments in stock market. Stock market volatility has long been a topic of interest for policy makers, market practitioners and academicians. It is a measure of how far the current prices of an asset deviates from its average past prices. Greater the deviation, greater is the volatility.

Volatility is defined as, "the degree to which the price of security, commodity, or the market rises or falls within a short term period". Volatility is defined in terms of statistical measures of the variability of percentage price change or rate of return. The most commonly used statistical measure of volatility is standard deviation of returns.

Standard deviation measures the dispersion of return or the degree to which they vary from period to period—the period being a month, day, hour or a minute.

10.3.1 Significance of Volatility Study

1. It is an indicator of market sentiments in stock market.
2. Market volatility is a measure of performance expectations for individual stocks and the broad economy.

Table 10.1: Important Measures of Risk in Stock Market

Measure	Description	Its Application
Alpha	Alpha measures risk relative to the market or a selected benchmark index. Negative alpha means investment is very risky given the return. An alpha of 0 suggests that investment has return commensurate with the risk. Alpha greater than 1 means investment has out-performed	If the stock outperforms the benchmark—positive alpha. If stock falls below the performance of the benchmark—negative alpha
Beta	It is used to measure the risk of an investment relative to the risk of a comparable market benchmark. In other words, it measures systematic risk	Betas below 1 are considered less volatile. Beta value more than 1 is considered more volatile
R-Squared	R-squared value represents the correlation between examined investment and its associated benchmark	R-squared value of 95—high correlation. R-squared value of 50—low correlation
Standard Deviation	Standard deviation tells how much an investment will fluctuate from the average return. It measures the total risk—systematic and unsystematic	Higher the standard deviation, higher the risk
Sharpe Ratio	Sharpe ratio is a measure for calculating risk-adjusted return	The greater the value of the Sharpe ratio, the more attractive the risk-adjusted return

3. Volatility influences the investment decision.
4. Volatility reflects changes in the local or global economic environment.
5. Volatility index is useful to determine the outlook of the investors in the market.

6. Volatility is the speed of price change of a stock. The more (excess) volatile a stock is, the more risky it is.
7. Excess volatility is undesirable and it can shake the confidence of an investor.

A market with lower volatility with other factors being constant would be more investor friendly and would attract larger and stable amount of capital. In addition, the cost of rising capital will also be low.

10.3.2 Factors Affecting Stock Market Volatility: Factors affecting stock market volatility can be classified into short-term and long-term.

A. Factors Affecting Long-term Volatility

(a) Operating Leverage: Larger operating leverage will translate the value of the firm more sensibly in relation to economic conditions. If the demand for a company's product falls off unexpectedly, the profits of the firms with large fixed costs will fall more than the profits of a firm that avoids large capital investments. In other words, long-term supply contracts with large fixed costs will have a higher stock return volatility. [3]

(b) Business Conditions: The ups and down in the economy would affect the volatility of stock returns. Stock volatility increases during an economic recession. A severe recession might lead to a sudden crisis arising out of the stock exchange. If recession continues for long, investment reduces to a very low level.

B. Factors Affecting Short-term Volatility

(a) Trading Volume: Trading volume is the number of stock that is traded. Trading activities and stock return volatility occurs together. Larger trading volume affects volatility. Generally, investors learn something by watching the stock prices set by the trading patterns of others. Thus, the use of stock price behaviour is an important input for trading strategies.

(b) Trading Halts: Trading halts may be applied in the form of circuit breakers and circuit filters. If investors tend to panic and overreact, a trading halt is implemented which reduces volatility. If some investors value liquidity very highly and fear that a trading halt will occur as prices approach the known limits, they will rush to sell to ensure their ability to trade. Such behaviour would speed up price declines and could lead to an overreaction. This would lead to increased volatility. It may also have an effect on lowering of prices of securities, perceived to be less liquid.

(c) Computerized Trading: Revolution in the IT sector and its application in stock market has changed the face of stock market and given it a fresh look. With greater use of information technology, stock trading has become quick, easier, wider and transparent. It has also brought an integration of stock markets among the nations. All these changes have affected the volatility of stock market/prices. Thus, computerized tools have made it easier to trade large amounts of stocks continuously.

(d) Noise Trading: Noise traders are economic agents who trade in securities market for non-information based reasons. Some investors may extrapolate recent changes in stock prices. Noise trading is trading on noise as if it was information and actually puts noise onto the prices. Thus, noise is essential for the existence of liquid market and changes the volatility of price (return).

(e) Political Uncertainty: Increasing political uncertainty in the market and socio-political instability also causes volatility. A stable government can take long-term decisions for economic development. Hence, stock markets always welcome a strong and stable government. A stable government can also increase international business confidence.

(f) International Linkages: With Indian markets integrating with global counterparts, international events too are influencing Indian stock prices significantly. For example, Brexit was a major event that caused a potential impact on the stock markets. Also, the stock market in general can be affected by world events such as war and civil unrest, natural disasters and terrorism.

(g) Market Makers: Market makers can create business by moving the stock prices. Some investors may react to change in stock prices in this way because they assume that other investors who are buying or selling stocks and causing the movement in stock prices have information about companies to which they do not have access. Thus, market makers have a role to play in volatile stock prices.

(h) Press/Media: It includes print media, electronic media, and social media being the important sources of information. Investors act as per the information given/shared by media. Thus, press information and comments may influence the timing of price changes with or without influencing the long-term movements.

(i) FII and Volatility: A significant improvement has taken place in India relating to the flow of foreign capital during the period of post-economic reforms. While welcoming the FIIs presence in the stock market, many analysts have opined that the elements of volatility have increased.

(j) Other Factors: Other factors such as instability of commodity prices, day trading, the low P/E effect, holidays, the January effect, the weekend effects etc. are some of factors causing volatility.

Thus, volatility process is driven by the simultaneous interaction of numerous components, associated with psychological factors, economic factors, social factors, political factors, and some unobserved factors.

10.3.3 Methods of Volatility Measurement in Stock Market: In stock market, volatility can be calculated as inter-day volatility and intra-day volatility. Standard deviation (**σ**) is a popular statistical measure of stock market volatility. It measures the amount of dispersion in a stock's price. Standard deviation rises as stock prices become more volatile. As stock prices calm, standard deviation heads lower.

A. Inter-day Volatility: The classical volatility estimators include close-close volatility and open-open volatility of select stocks. The variation in stock price return between two trading days is called inter-day volatility. Inter-day volatility is calculated by logarithmic returns of:

- Close to close share price of BSE indices, and
- Open to open share price of BSE indices.

(a) Close to Close Volatility: It is termed as historical volatility. It is the most commonly used measure of volatility. For calculating close to close volatility, the closing prices of the BSE-SENSEX, BSE-100, BSE-200 and BSE-500 are taken. Close to close volatility is measured as follows: [4]

$$\sigma = \sqrt{(1/n-1)\sum\left(r_t - \bar{r}\right)^2}$$

Where,

n = Number of trading days

r_t = Close to close return (in natural log)

r = Average of close to close return

(b) Open to Open Volatility: Stock market participants are also interested in open to open volatility because opening prices of shares reflect a positive or negative information that arrives after the close of the market and before the start of next day's trading. The following formula [5] is used to calculate open to open volatility.

$$\sigma = \sqrt{(1/n-1)\sum\left(r_t - \bar{r}\right)^2}$$

Where,

N= number of trading days

r_t= open to open returns (in natural log)

= Average of the open to open return

B. Intra-day Volatility: So far, inter-day volatility is calculated by computing close to close index level on daily basis. For many fund managers, investors, regulators and policy makers, intra-day volatility has assumed considerable significance because of its influence on the decision of the market participants and its impact on other instruments such as derivatives. Several metrics are employed to estimate intra-day volatility.

C. **Parkinson Estimator** [6]**:** The Parkinson volatility measure was developed by physicist Michael Parkinson in

1980. It is a volatility measure that considers the securities' high and low price during the day. High-low volatility is calculated by using following formula:

$$\sigma = k\sqrt{1/n\sum \log(H_t / L_t)^2}$$

Where,

σ = High-low volatility

K = 0.601

H_t = High price on the day

L_t = Low price on the day

n = Number of trading days

The basic difference between classical volatility measures and Parkinson volatility is that, the latter uses high and low stock prices for a day, rather than the closing or opening stock prices.

"An important use of the Parkinson number is the assessment of the distribution prices during the day as well as a better understanding of the market dynamics.

Comparing the Parkinson number and periodically sampled volatility helps traders understand the tendency towards mean reversion in the market as well as the distribution of stop-losses". [7]

D. Garman and Klass Model [8]: Garman Klass is a volatility estimator that combines open, low, high, and close prices of a stock. The formula for Garman and Klass model is as follows.

$$\sigma = \sqrt{(1/n)\sum(1/2)[\log(H_t/L_t)]^2 - [2\log(2)-1][\log(C_t/O_t)]^2}$$

Where,

σ = Intra-day volatility for the period

H_t = High price on the day

O_t = Opening price on the day

C_t = Closing price on the day

L_t = Low price on the day

Garman Klass volatility is calculated by multiplying the return value by the square root of the number of trading periods in a year.

Garman Klass is a volatility estimator which includes open, low, high, and close prices of a share. In short, Garman-Klass volatility extends Parkinson's volatility by taking into account the opening and closing stock prices.

10.4 Seasonality in Stock Market

It is also observed that seasonality affects stock market significantly. There are times in the year when the stock market does well and then there are other times when stock market under-performs.

Seasonality is a common tendency of human behaviour and stock market is not an exception to it.

Seasonality is a characteristic of time-series analysis. It is a situation where the data experiences regular and predictable changes that recur every calendar year.

Generally, there are three types of seasonality experienced in the stock market:

- Weekend effect,
- Monthly effect, and
- Holiday effect.

In addition to this, we can experience the following types of seasonality in Indian stock market also:

- Year-end effect,
- January effect,
- Budget effect, and
- Diwali effect.

Endnotes

1. B.J. Queensly Jayanthi (2010), "A Study of NSE in India", Serials Publication, New Delhi, p. 101.
2. Harvindar Kaur (2002), "Stock Market Volatility in India", Deep and Deep Publications, New Delhi, p. 2.
3. Ibid.
4. B.J. Queensly Jayanthi (2010), "A Study of NSE in India", op. cit., p. 111.
5. Ibid.
6. SEBI, "Annual Report, 2002-03", p. 56.

7. Nissim Taleb (1997), "Dynamic Hedging: Managing Vanilla and Exotic Options", John Wiley & sons Inc., New York.

11

Macroeconomic Variables and Stock Market

Everything in financial markets is connected with each other. Therefore, understanding relationship between macroeconomic variables and stock market is an important matter for investment decisions. Macroeconomic variables are the broad indicators of economic growth. GDP, interest rates, inflation, foreign capital flows, trade, money supply, index of industrial production (IIP) and exchange rate are important fundamental macroeconomic variables. Generally, stock prices are determined by some macroeconomic variables. These fundamental variables can influence investors' investment decision in the capital market. In short, it affects the performance of the stock market. A number of studies in the past have been conducted to determine the relationship between fundamental macroeconomic variables and equity prices. Let us understand the relationship between macroeconomic variables and stock market.

11.1 Gross Domestic Product (GDP) and Stock Market

GDP growth rate is an important indicator of the economic performance of a country. There are different concepts of national income including GDP, GNP and NNP, etc. GDP is widely used as a traditional measure to determine the size of an economy. GDP is defined as 'the final value of the goods and services produced within the geographical boundaries of a country during a specified period of time, normally a year'. Thus, growth in the economy is measured by growth in the real gross domestic product.

GDP is calculated at current (nominal) prices and constant prices. To determine 'real' GDP, its nominal value must be adjusted for inflation, to reflect changes in real output, through which one can understand whether the value of output has increased because more is being produced or simply because prices have increased. Therefore, a statistical tool called 'price deflator' is used to adjust GDP from nominal to constant prices.

Various well-known economists and researchers are suspicious of the idea that stock market is a crucial factor in the development of an economy. Robinson, a well-known British economist, supported the idea that financial markets do not indicate economic growth. Kuznets in his research stated that stock markets start to expand till the national economy advances towards the halfway level of the expansion activity and evolve as soon as the economy has fully grown. So, this meant that in a developing or an under-developed economy, the financial market would not grow as the economy grows.

11.2 Interest Rates and Stock Market

Interest rate is the cost of borrowing money, and also it is the money which is earned from savings. Interest rate is determined by a nation's central bank that controls the money supply in the economy as well as the banking sector. The central bank usually regulates the interest rate quarterly to stabilize inflation and control the country's exchange rates. There are two different types of interest rates: nominal interest rate and real interest rate. A nominal interest rate refers to the interest rate without taking inflation into account. Generally, it is the interest rate quoted on bonds and loans, while real interest rate is the interest rate corrected for the effects of inflation.

In theory, relationship between interest rate and stock market is negative. This is due to the cash flow discounting model according to which, present value of stocks are calculated by discounting the future cash flow at a discount rate. If discount rate increases, the present value of stocks decline and vice-versa. Apart from this, there are other reasons also which account for a negative relationship between interest rates and stock prices. First, interest rates are risk free returns on bonds and as interest rates on bonds rise, bonds become more attractive and stocks less attractive. Consequently, there is a change in asset allocation in favour of bonds rather than stocks. This moves funds from the stock market to the bond market, which invariably increases the demand for bonds and reduces the demand for stocks. Second, corporate profitability is hit by an increase in the interest rates in two ways: (i) companies' earnings fall, and (ii) with an increase in the interest rate, cost of borrowing goes up which leaves consumers with less cash in hand, affecting the demand negatively. As demand declines, sales also decline. With decrease in profitability, stock prices also decline and vice-versa.

Looking from the practical point of view, RBI sets the repo rate as a part of its monetary policy. The repo rate becomes the benchmark rate and commercial banks in the country decide about borrowing rates for businesses and people, based on this benchmark rate. Therefore, stock markets watch out for the monetary policy of the Reserve Bank of India. In short, interest rates affect stock markets directly and indirectly in the following ways.

1. High interest rate hurts profits of the companies.
2. Small and medium sized companies are hit hardest due to high interest rates.
3. High interest rates reduce domestic participation in capital market.
4. Future growth of companies and expansion is also affected due to persistent high interest rates.

In short, interest rate is very crucial for how the market reacts. If interest rate is attractive, people will withdraw their money from the stock market and park their investments in safe and risk-free fixed earning instruments. If RBI keeps interest rates low, reverse will happen in the financial markets. If FED of US increases interest rate, FIIs start withdrawing their funds from the Indian stock markets and create a selling pressure in Indian stock market which pushes the stock market down and creates a panic movement for the domestic investors.

11.3 Inflation and Stock Market

Inflation is monetary phenomena. It is measured as the rate of change of prices of goods and services that households buy. In India, inflation is mainly measured by two main indices i.e. CPI (consumer price index) and WPI (wholesale price index). Consumer price index measures the percentage change in the price of basket of goods and services consumed by households. On the other hand, goods or services sold by businesses to businesses for selling further, is taken by the WPI. Inflation is one of those macroeconomic phenomena that affect every citizen, almost every day.

Inflation is a double-edged sword for the stock market, i.e., it has a positive as well a negative impact on the stock market. Inflation has a positive impact on cyclical stocks suggesting that demand persists in the market. The cyclical stocks are those stocks which tend to do well when the economy is growing and tend to do bad when the economy is falling. But looking into the negative effects, inflation can increase the price of raw materials, which will have a negative impact on the cash flow of a company. The most important thing is that inflation is accompanied by increasing interest rates. It is done by the RBI to prevent economy from inflation. If interest rate goes up, investors' expectations for returns increases as risk free rate of return has increased. Also, rise in interest rate on debt instruments by RBI basically means investors want more returns from the equity segment. For example, if inflation rate is 6.0%, investors in stock market would expect returns more than that, say 8.0%. In short, investors in stock market would always try to beat inflation.

Following points show how interest rates affect equity markets in India.

1. Inflation impacts stock market via interest rate.
2. Inflation impacts the purchasing power of investors.
3. Inflation impacts stock valuation.

11.4 Index of Industrial Production (IIP) and Stock Market

It is an index which shows the growth rates in different

industry groups of an economy over a period of time. It is a key economic indicator of the manufacturing sector of an economy. It is a composite indicator that measures the growth rate of industry groups.

This indicator measures short-term changes in the volume of production of industrial products in a country with reference to a base period. IIP considers eight core sectors of Indian economy such as coal, crude oil, natural gas, refinery products, fertilizers, steel, cement and electricity. IIP gives the overall picture of production activity in a country and there is ample literature to demonstrate the impact of IIP on stock market. The movement of index of industrial production (IIP) is gaining importance because better IIP figures bring in hope and optimism in the stock market in general and among investors in particular. Thus, IIP affects the sentiments of investors in the stock market. Generally, lower IIP is bad news for the stock market as well as for the growth of the economy.

11.5 Foreign Capital and Stock Market

India has emerged as one of the most favoured destinations for global investors. The number of FIIs registered with SEBI has gone up significantly. Foreign portfolio investors have been one of the largest drivers of Indian stock market. Foreign institutional investors (FIIs), non-resident Indians (NRIs), and persons of Indian origin (PIOs) are allowed to invest in the primary and secondary market in India under the Portfolio Investment Scheme (PIS). Under this scheme, FIIs/NRIs can acquire shares/debentures of Indian companies through stock exchanges in India. Indian stock market is quite dominated by FIIs and its inflow (buying pressure) and outflow (selling pressure) directly affects the Indian stock market. Looking into size of FIIs in Indian stock market, and compared with total market capitalisation, FIIs holding was around 20 percent in 2021.

Foreign institutional investors consider 'opportunity cost' of their investments in Indian stock market. It is calculated by comparing the returns from different emerging economies. The stock market moves up when FIIs pour money and falls when they book profit. Along with returns from the stock market, foreign investors also consider regulatory framework of emerging economies and accordingly park their money.

11.6 Exchange Rate and Stock Market

Stock prices are affected by multiple factors out of which exchange rate fluctuations is an important one. Exchange rate is defined as, the price of one currency in terms of another currency. Forex rate can be either fixed or floating. Fixed exchange rates are decided by central banks of a country whereas floating (flexible) exchange rates are decided by the mechanism of market demand and supply in the foreign exchange market. In short, exchange rate is an effective tool to calculate and compare the value of domestic currency with the value of foreign currency and domestic goods prices with international prices.

The relationship between exchange rate and stock market may vary from country to country. It may be different depending upon domestic economic conditions, import-export conditions and relations with the global world. Relationship between exchange rate and stock market can be understood by considering the possibility of depreciation and appreciation of domestic currency. A depreciation of the domestic currency makes exporting goods more attractive and leads to an increase in foreign demand and resultantly greater revenue for the firm. It consequently leads to appreciation in value and hence the stock price. Contrarily, an appreciation of the local currency decreases profits of the exporting firm because it leads to a decrease in foreign demand for its products. In short, the impact of exchange rate fluctuations on stock market depends on two factors viz., the importance of a country's international trade in its economy and the degree of trade imbalance.

On the other hand, according to portfolio balance approach, a prospering stock market of a country would attract foreign capital flows, which may cause an increase in the demand for a country's currency. The reverse would happen in case of falling stock prices where the investors would try to sell their stocks to avoid further losses and would convert their money into their currency to move out of the country.

11.7 Money Supply and Stock Market

Money supply is the stock of money in the economy which is issued by a country's monetary authority (central bank). It is also called as the total amount of money available in an economy at a particular point of time.

The competing theories to be examined here are the ones developed by the Keynesian economists and the real activity theorists. Keynesian economists argue that there is a negative relationship between stock prices and money supply whereas real activity theorists argue that the relationship between the two variables is positive.

In other words, there is a mixed opinion among different economists about stock prices and money supply relationship. The Keynesian hypothesis predicts that in response to announcement of an unexpected increase in the money supply, stock prices will decline.

Recent empirical studies suggest that monetary policy has a significant impact on stock market returns. Nowadays, monetary authorities are following the policy of 'monetary easing' (i.e. printing new money) as a solution for overcoming economic crises. As government pumps lots of money into economy, it brings more money in the hands of people and their demand for goods and services go up constantly. This creates a demand pull inflationary situation.

If high inflation rate happens, the resulting interest rates might go up. Thus, putting more money into the system creates inflationary pressure in an economy and to arrest inflation, monetary authority increase interest rates. Thus, a rise in interest rates directly affects the stock market significantly.

11.8 Fiscal Policy and Stock Market

Fiscal policy is related to changes in government spending and revenue behaviour in an effort to influence the economy. By adjusting its level of public spending and tax revenue, the government can affect economic activities by either increasing or decreasing the economic activity.

The Keynesian hypothesis centres on the use of automatic stabiliser and discretionary measures by fiscal authorities in such ways that support aggregate demand, boosts economy and of course increase stock prices. The hypothesis believes that effects of fiscal policy instruments on stock market are positive as fiscal policy makers can use budget deficit, tax and other discretionary measures, to alter the interest rate, thereby improving stock market performance. For example, increase in public expenditure will result in increased money supply thus affecting the stock market positively.

Stock market performance, pre- and post-budget is an important event for the analysts. Investors in the equity market wait for the budget announcements so that they can take an informed decision to invest in the stock market.

To sum up, everything in the financial markets is connected with each other. There is a 'vicious circle' of relation between macroeconomic factors and stock prices. The volatility of stock market in general and stock prices in particular is significantly affected by performance of macroeconomic indicators, but the intensity of impact varies from country to country. Therefore, analysts and investors should take into account, movements in macroeconomic forces and behaviour of stock prices.

12

Regulatory Framework for Stock Market

Stock market is not a gambling place, but it is a well organised and regulated market. A well regulated market has the prospective to boost additional investors to participate, and contribute in, promoting development of the economy. Stock market has a legal status and its activities come under the purview of certain rules and regulations. Every market player or participant has to follow certain pre-designed market disciplines. Either it is the primary market or the secondary market certain rules have to be followed. Every investor should know about its legal structure. In this chapter, an attempt is made to outline the regulatory framework for Indian stock market.

Indian stock market is regulated and monitored by four major entities. These are the following:

1. Ministry of Finance, Government of India.
2. Reserve Bank of India (RBI).
3. Securities and Exchange Board of India (SEBI).
4. Stock exchanges viz., BSE and NSE of India Ltd. (Figure 12.1).

12.1 Ministry of Finance

The work of the Ministry is divided into 5 departments.

12.1.1 Department of Economic Affairs (DEA): DEA is the nodal agency of the Union Government to formulate and monitor country's economic policies and programmes having a bearing on domestic and international aspects of economic management.

A principal responsibility of this Department is the preparation of the Union Budget annually. Other main functions include the following:

Figure 12.1: Stock Market Regulators in India

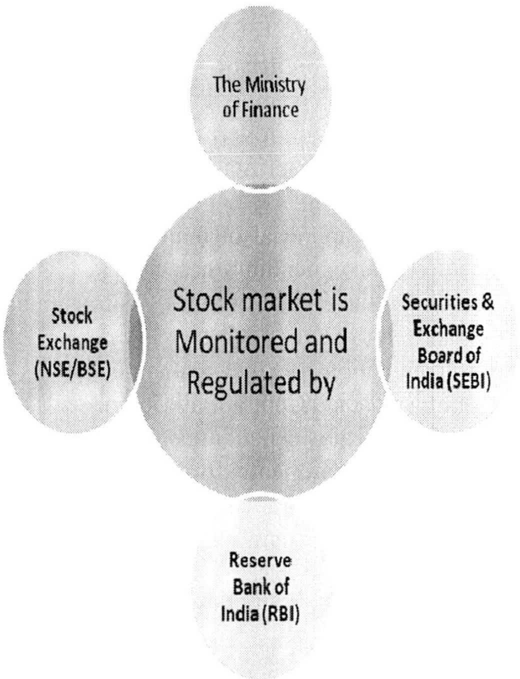

1. Formulation and monitoring of macroeconomic policies, including issues relating to fiscal policy and public finance, inflation, public debt management and the functioning of capital market including stock exchanges. In this context, it looks at ways and means to raise internal resources through taxation, market borrowings and mobilization of small savings.
2. Monitoring and raising of external resources through multilateral and bilateral official development assistance (ODA), sovereign borrowings abroad, foreign investments and monitoring foreign exchange resources including balance of payments.
3. Production of bank notes and coins of various

denominations, postal stationery, postal stamps; cadre management, career planning and training of the Indian Economic Service (IES) officers.

12.1.2 Department of Expenditure: It is the nodal Department for overseeing the public financial management system of the Central Government and matters connected with State finances. The principal activities of the Department include the following:

1. Pre-sanction appraisal of major schemes/projects (both Plan and non-Plan expenditure).
2. Handling the bulk of the Central budgetary resources transferred to States.
3. Implementation of the recommendations of the Finance Commission and Central Pay Commission.
4. Overseeing the expenditure management in the Central Ministries/Departments through the interface with the financial advisors and the administration of the financial rules, regulations and orders through monitoring of audit comments and observations.
5. Preparation of Central Government Accounts.
6. Managing the financial aspects of personnel management in the Central Government.
7. Assisting Central Ministries/Departments in controlling the costs and prices of public services.
8. Assisting organizational re-engineering through review of staffing patterns and reviewing systems and procedures to optimize outputs and outcomes of public expenditure.

The Department also coordinates matters concerning the Ministry of Finance including Parliament-related work of the Ministry. The Department has under its administrative control the National Institute of Financial Management (NIFM), Faridabad.

12.1.3 Department of Revenue: It exercises control in respect of matters relating to all the direct and indirect Union taxes through two statutory Boards namely, the Central Board of Direct Taxes (CBDT) and the Central Board of Excise and

Customs (CBEC). Each Board is headed by a chairman who is also ex-officio Special Secretary to the Government of India. Matters relating to the levy and collection of all Direct taxes are looked after by the CBDT whereas those relating to levy and collection of Customs and Central Excise duties and other Indirect taxes fall within the purview of the CBEC. The two Boards were constituted under the Central Board of Revenue Act, 1963.

12.1.4 Department of Financial Services: It looks after the following matters:

1. Citizen's Charter.
2. Banking.
3. Industrial finance and micro small and medium enterprise sector.
4. Insurance.
5. Pension reforms.
6. Work allocation.
7. Advertisements.

12.1.5 Department of Investment and Public Asset Management: It promotes people's ownership of Central Public Sector Enterprises to share in their prosperity through disinvestment. The Mission of the Department is as follows:

1. List all profitable Central Public Sector Enterprises (CPSEs) on stock exchanges.
2. Listing to result in: (a) improvement in corporate governance, (b) higher disclosure levels due to listing to bring about greater transparency and accountability in the functioning of the CPSEs, and (c) adding market discipline to the functioning of CPSEs
3. Disinvestment process to facilitate unlocking the true value of the CPSEs for all stakeholders—investors, employees, company and the Government.

12.2 Reserve Bank of India (RBI)

There is only one central bank in a country whose main function is to control the operations of the rest of the banking system. Reserve Bank of India (RBI), the central bank of India, is the apex institution responsible for managing and supervising the monetary and financial system of the economy.

RBI performs all the major functions of a central bank and these are discussed below.

12.2.1 Sole Currency Authority: The management of currency is one of the core functions of a central bank and one, which commands a high degree of public visibility. This is especially so in a country like India, where people have a marked preference for cash transactions. The fact that there are a number of inaccessible pockets in the country adds to the already formidable challenges in managing currency in India.

In terms of the RBI Act, the affairs of the RBI relating to note issue and general banking business are conducted separately through Issue Department and Banking Department. The Issue Department is responsible for the aggregate value of the currency notes of the RBI in circulation from time to time and maintains the eligible assets for equivalent value. The mechanism of putting currency into circulation and its withdrawal from circulation (expansion and contraction of currency) is undertaken through the Banking Department.

Barring one-rupee notes and coins, RBI is the sole authority for the issue of currency in India. One rupee notes and coins are issued by the Central Government. However, their distribution to the public is the sole responsibility of the RBI. For the issue of notes, the RBI has a separate department, the Department of Issue. All the currency issued by the RBI is its monetary liability and is backed by assets of equal value.

Currency management by the RBI is currently passing through a modernisation phase. A number of significant steps have been taken in this sphere which includes the following.

1. Building up of the capacity of note printing presses.
2. Reforms in the operations of the Issue Department including in the note distribution network.
3. Introduction of new security features.
4. Shift towards higher denomination notes in circulation.

12.2.2 Banker to the Governments: Before the formation of the RBI, the Imperial Bank of India performed many of the functions as banker to the Government. With the establishment of the RBI, the Imperial Bank ceased to be the banker to the Government, but entered into an agreement with the RBI for providing its services as the sole agent of the RBI in places where it had a branch and there was no branch of the Banking Department of the RBI.

As the banker to the Central Government and to the State Governments by virtue of agreements entered into with them, the RBI provides a range of banking services for these Governments such as acceptance of money on government account payment/withdrawals of funds and collection and transfer of funds through different means. Sections 20, 21 and 21A of the RBI Act provide the statutory basis for these functions. The terms and conditions on which the RBI acts as banker to the Central and State Governments are set out in separate agreements, which the RBI entered into with these Governments.

Presently, RBI is the banker for all Governments in India (except Jammu and Kashmir). The RBI provides all those banking services to the Central and State Governments which a commercial bank ordinarily offers to its customers. The Governments keep their cash balances on current account deposit with the RBI and the latter carries out banking business involving receipts and payments of money on behalf of the Governments. The Governments are required, under agreement, to maintain a minimum balance with the RBI. It is the duty of the Finance Department of each Government to ensure that there are always sufficient funds in its bank account and that at no stage the cash balance falls short of the prescribed minimum.

12.2.3 Bankers' Bank and Lender-of-the-last-resort: Under the Reserve Bank of India Act, 1934 and the Banking Regulation Act, 1949, the RBI is vested with extensive powers of supervision, regulation, and control over commercial and co-operative banks. The regulatory functions of the RBI pertain to licensing, branch expansion, and amalgamation of commercial banks. The RBI calls for returns and other information from the commercial banks and periodically inspects their working.

The scheduled banks in India are required under law to deposit with the RBI a stipulated ratio (lying between 3 percent and 15 percent) of their total liabilities. These are compulsory reserves of banks with the RBI and are not available to them for meeting inter-bank clearing claims. The underlying philosophy of this statutory reserve requirement is that by varying it within limits, the RBI can use it as a weapon of monetary-credit control.

Reserves of the banks with the RBI may be used to meet the temporary cash needs of the commercial banks. Commercial banks are supposed to meet their shortfalls of cash from sources other than the RBI but in acute emergency they can approach the RBI for help and that is why the central bank is also called the lender-of-the-last-resort.

12.2.4 Controller of Money and Credit: Like other central banks, the core function of the RBI is to formulate and administer monetary policy to maintain the stability of the rupee. During Pre-Independence period, there was, however, no formal monetary policy formulation other than that of administering the supply and demand for credit in the economy. The Bank Rate [1], reserve requirements and open market operations [2] were the mechanisms for regulating the credit availability. The Bank Rate, as an instrument of control, was not used at all in this period, except once in November 1935 when the rate was reduced from 3.5 percent to 3.0 percent. The rate remained unchanged thereafter till November 1951. The RBI, however, employed the instruments of open market operations (OMOs) in a fairly substantial way. Although the RBI was vested with adequate powers to resort to the qualitative instruments, *viz.* selective credit control, no need was felt during the initial stages of its functioning due to the existence of price stability.

The RBI has multiple instruments at its command such as repo and reverse repo rates [3], cash reserve ratio (CRR), statutory liquidity ratio (SLR), open market operations, including the market stabilisation scheme (MSS) and the liquidity adjustment facility (LAF), special market operations, and sector-specific liquidity facilities. In addition, the RBI also uses prudential tools to modulate flow of credit to certain sectors consistent with financial stability. The availability of multiple instruments and flexible use of these instruments in the implementation of monetary policy has enabled the RBI to modulate the liquidity and interest rate conditions amidst uncertain global macroeconomic conditions.

An important function of RBI is to control money and credit in the country. The instruments of monetary control operated by the RBI may be classified into two categories: (a) quantitative or global or aggregative measures which affect the total amount of money supply and credit and (b) qualitative or selective measures which affect the allocation of bank credit among competing uses and users.

12.2.5 Controller of Foreign Exchange: The RBI is the custodian of the foreign exchange reserves of India. It manages exchange control and the external value of the rupee. The history of exchange control in India dates back to the outbreak of Second World War in 1939. The exchange control is operated in a manner so that the demand for foreign exchange is contained within the limits of its available supplies. In other words, the available foreign exchange is allocated among competing demands in such a way as to make its optimum use. The need for this control and planned use arises in view of the general shortage of foreign exchange reserves in most developing countries. All foreign exchange transactions made by the RBI are at the official rates of exchange.

The RBI has delegated considerable powers to the authorised dealers to release foreign exchange for a variety of purposes and has been focusing on the development of the foreign exchange market. In order to deepen the foreign exchange market, a large number of products have been introduced and the entry of newer players has been allowed. Additional hedging instruments, such as, foreign currency-rupee options have been introduced and authorised dealers have been permitted to use innovative products like cross-currency options, interest rate and currency swaps, caps/collars and forward rate agreements (FRAs) in the international forex market.

12.3 Securities and Exchange Board of India (SEBI)

The Securities and Exchange Board of India (SEBI) was constituted on April 12, 1988 as a non-statutory body through an Administrative Resolution of the Government for dealing with all matters relating to development and regulation of the securities market and investor protection and to advise the government on all these matters. SEBI was given statutory status and powers through an Ordinance promulgated on January 30, 1992. SEBI was established as a statutory body on February 21, 1992. The Ordinance was replaced by Securities and Exchange Board of India Act, 1992 on April 4, 1992.

In 1992, the Capital Issues (Control) Act, 1947 was repealed and the office of the Controller of Capital Issues (CCIs) was abolished. With this ended all controls related to raising of funds from the market. The move was aimed at enhancing the efficiency, safety, integrity and transparency of the market. Presently, issuers of capital are required to meet the guidelines of SEBI on disclosures and protection of investors.

In short, though SEBI was originally set up in 1988, it did not have any legal status to control securities market transactions. Legal Status was granted to SEBI in 1992 to help it curb malpractices in securities market like rigging of stock prices, insider trading, pricing of new issues without any basis, etc.

12.3.1 Objectives of SEBI: SEBI has emerged as an autonomous and independent statutory body. Its legally mandated objectives are the following:

1. Development of the securities market.
2. Regulation of the securities market activities.
3. Protection of the interests of investors in securities.
4. Prevention of malpractices.
5. Code of conduct for intermediaries.
6. Matters connected therewith and incidental thereto.

SEBI prohibits fraudulent and unfair trade practices, including insider trading. It also regulates substantial acquisition of shares and takeovers. In order to ensure protection of investors and to safeguard the integrity of the markets, there is a comprehensive surveillance system. Stock exchanges are the primary targets for detection of market manipulation, price rigging and other regulatory breaches regarding capital market functioning.

12.3.2 Functions of SEBI: SEBI performs the following functions:

A. Protective Functions:

1. Preventing price rigging.
2. Curbing insider trading.
3. Checking fraudulent and unfair trade practices.
4. Developing and monitoring investor grievance redressal mechanism.
5. Initiating punitive action against erring entities.

B. Developmental Functions:

1. Certification for intermediaries.
2. Technology adoption for faster business.
3. Investment products.

C. Regulatory Functions:

1. Registration of intermediaries.
2. Framing rules for intermediary operations.
3. Regulation of mutual funds.

12.3.3 Powers of SEBI: SEBI regulates and supervises the securities market through its various regulations, guidelines and schemes issued from time-to-time.

Powers and functions of SEBI—as the securities market regulator—have been laid down in the SEBI Act, 1992. SEBI also exercises powers under the Securities Contracts (Regulation) Act, 1956, the Depositories Act, 1996 and certain provisions of the Companies Act, 1956. It regulates the securities markets, securities market institutions and market intermediaries such as the stock exchanges, depositories, mutual funds and other asset management companies, securities dealers and brokers, merchant bankers, credit rating agencies and venture capital funds.

The statutory powers and functions of SEBI were strengthened through the promulgation of the Securities Laws (Amendment) Ordinance on January 25, 1995, which was subsequently replaced by an Act of Parliament.

The SEBI is equipped with the following powers:

1. Powers to register and regulate, inspect, enquire and investigate and undertake audits, and to cancel registration (though in this last case this applies to the mutual fund rather than the AMC); also to prohibit issue of an offer document including prospectus or advertisement.
2. Powers to summon and enforce attendance and examine on oath, inspect registers and documents, discover and enforce disclosure of books of account and other documents.
3. Powers to restrain from business, suspend, search, impound and retain proceeds, access bank data and attach bank accounts, prevent alienation of assets and issue cease and desist orders.
4. Powers to require compensation to be paid to investors.

SEBI has the power to impose penalties for violation of the Act and Regulations made under the Act. The Act empowers SEBI to investigate, adjudicate, hold enquiry and prosecute. There are also general powers to pass directions against listed companies in the interest of investors or the orderly development of securities market.

SEBI has around 980 staff and regional offices in five cities, viz. Mumbai, New Delhi, Chennai, Kolkata and Ahmedabad.

The experience of SEBI during episodes of market misconduct revealed many limitations in the legal provisions of the SEBI Act. In addition, the growing importance of the securities markets in the economy has placed new demands upon SEBI. On October 28, 2002, an ordinance was promulgated which sought to strengthen SEBI. This ordinance involved organisational strengthening of SEBI, giving SEBI more powers for investigations and penalties, and making clearer concepts like insider trading and market manipulations.

The regulatory ambit has been widened in tune with the emerging needs and developments in the equity markets. Apart from stock exchanges, various intermediaries such as mutual funds, stock brokers and sub-brokers, merchant bankers, portfolio managers, registrars to an issue, share transfer agents, underwriters, debentures trustees, bankers to an issue, custodian of securities, venture capital funds and issuers have been brought under the SEBI's regulatory purview.

12.3.4 Model Listing Agreement: Listing agreement is an agreement entered between a stock exchange and the company seeking listing of securities on the exchange. It contains various requirements and disclosure obligations that companies must follow to remain as listed entities.

The Model Listing Agreement has been stipulated by SEBI and is reviewed and amended by SEBI from time-to-time.

Clause 49 of the Listing Agreement of SEBI requires the companies, who are listed, to comply with certain provisions relating to board of directors, audit committee, subsidiary companies, disclosures, report on corporate governance and compliance.

Stock exchanges are primarily responsible for ensuring compliance of various requirements under Listing Agreement.

Securities Contracts (Regulation) Act (SCRA), 1956 stipulates penalties up to ` 25 crore for non-compliance of listing conditions pursuant to adjudication by an adjudicating officer appointed by SEBI.

12.3.5 Appeals against SEBI Judgements: Those who

appeal against SEBI judgements are heard by the Securities Appellate Tribunal (SAT) and can also go to the Supreme Court if they do not accept the Tribunal's judgement. The SAT has three members, one of whom is required to be the presiding officer who is a sitting or retired judge of the Supreme Court or High Court. The two other members must be of ability, integrity and standing with experience of corporate law, securities law, finance, economics or accountancy.

12.3.6 Merger of Forward Markets Commission with SEBI: Forward Markets Commission for the purpose of regulating commodity futures market was merged with SEBI in September 2015.

12.4 Stock Exchanges (NSE/BSE)

According to section 9 of the Securities Contracts (Regulation) Act, 1956; any recognised stock exchanges (BSE/NSE), make by-laws for the regulation and control of contracts at stock exchanges. Some important by-laws are the following:

1. The opening and closing of stock markets and the regulation of the hours of trade.
2. The listing and delisting norms of securities on the stock exchange,
3. The procedure for the settlement of claims or disputes, including settlement by arbitration.
4. A clearing house for the periodical settlement of contracts
5. The levy and recovery of fees, fines and penalties;
6. The fixing of a rules of brokerage and other charges

Endnotes

1. Bank Rate is defined as the standard rate at which the RBI is prepared to buy or discount the bills of exchange or other commercial paper eligible for purchase under Section 49 of the RBI Act.
2. Open Market Operations refer to buying and selling of securities by the RBI, particularly from/to the scheduled commercial banks, as part of the policy to maintain orderly coordination in the securities market.

3. Repo (Repurchase Option) Operations: RBI is able to influence short-term interest rates by modulating the liquidity in the system through repo operations under the liquidity adjustment facility (LAF), reinforced by interest rate signals. RBI enforces the interest rate corridor defined by the reverse repo rate, i.e. the price at which it absorbs liquidity and the repo rate/bank rate, i.e. the price at which it injects liquidity into the system. In other words, repo rate is the rate at which RBI repurchases government securities from banks. In return, banks get cash to meet their short-term requirements. When RBI wants to inject liquidity in the system it reduces the repo rate which also acts as the benchmark short-term lending rate.

13

Legal Framework for Stock Market

13.1 Securities Contracts (Regulation) Act (SCRA), 1956

SCRA regulates transactions in securities. The Act deals with recognition of stock exchanges by Central Government (whose powers in this case are delegated to SEBI), powers to suspend the business of stock exchange or supersede its governing board. It provides for regulation of contracts and options in securities. There are also provisions relating to listing of securities and right to appeal to Securities Appellate Tribunal in case of refusal by exchange to list securities of listed companies. Under the Act, there are provisions for adjudication proceedings to be conducted by adjudicating officer appointed by SEBI and imposition of monetary penalties for various violations. SEBI also has powers to issue directions against entities such as stock exchanges, listed companies etc. There are also provisions for initiation of prosecution proceedings under the Act.

Central Government has also issued Securities Contracts (Regulation) Rules, 1957 which, *inter alia*, contain qualifications for persons to be members of stock exchange, books of accounts to be maintained by members, listing conditions etc.

Stock exchanges in India are regulated and controlled by the Securities Contracts (Regulation) Act, 1956. The objects clause describes the Act as "An Act to prevent undesirable transactions in securities by regulating the business of dealing therein, by providing for certain other matters connected therewith".

13.1.1 Meaning of Securities and Government Securities: Under Section 2 of the Securities Contracts (Regulation) Act, 1956, securities includes the following:

1. Shares, scrips, stocks, bonds, debentures, debenture stocks, or other marketable securities of a like nature in or of any incorporated company or other body corporate.
2. Government securities.
3. Such other instruments as may be declared by the Central Govt. to be securities.
4. Rights or interests in securities.

Government Securities mean securities created and issued—whether before or after the commencement of the Securities Contracts (Regulations) Act, 1956—by the Central Government or a State Government for the purpose of raising a public loan and having one of the forms specified in Section 2(2) of the Public Debt Act, 1944 (since replaced by the Government Securities Act, 2006).

13.1.2 Meaning and Recognition of Stock Exchange: According to the Act, stock exchange means any body of individuals, whether incorporated or not, constituted for the purpose of assisting, regulating or controlling the business of buying, selling or dealing in securities. Any stock exchange, which is desirous of being recognised for the purposes of this Act may make an application in the prescribed manner to the Government (Section 3). The Central Government may grant recognition to a stock exchange if it is satisfied, after making such inquiry as may be necessary in this behalf and after obtaining such further information, if any, as it may require (Section 4).

If the Central Government is of the opinion that the recognition granted to a stock exchange under the provisions of this Act should, in the interest of the trade or in the public interest, be withdrawn, the Central Government may serve on the governing body of the stock exchange a written notice that the Central Government is considering withdrawal of recognition for the reasons stated in the notice and after giving an opportunity to the governing body to be heard in the matter, the Central Government may withdraw, by notification in Official Gazette, the recognition granted to the stock exchange (Section 5).

13.1.3 Amendment of Securities Contract Regulation Act (SCRA): In pursuance of the recommendations of the L.C. Gupta Committee, SCRA was amended in December 1999 to include derivatives within the ambit of *securities* and the regulatory framework was developed for governing derivatives trading. The Act also made it clear that derivatives shall be legal and valid only if such contracts are traded on a recognised stock exchange, thus precluding OTC derivatives. The government also rescinded in March 2000, the three-decade old notification, which prohibited forward trading in securities.

Derivatives trading commenced in India in June 2000 after SEBI granted the final approval to this effect in May 2000. SEBI permitted the derivatives segments of two stock exchanges NSE and BSE, and their clearing house/corporation to commence trading and settlement in approved derivative contracts. To begin with, SEBI approved trading in index future contracts based on S&P CNX Nifty and BSE-30 (Sensex) index. This was followed by approval for trading in options which commenced in June 2001 and the trading in options on individual securities commenced in July 2001. Future contracts on individual stocks were launched in November 2001. Trading and settlement in derivative contracts is done in accordance with the rules, by-laws, and regulations of the respective exchanges and their clearing house/corporation duly approved by SEBI and notified in the official gazette.

13.2 Depositories Act, 1996 and Depositories and Participants Regulations, 2018

Depository Act, 1996 provides for regulation of depositories in securities markets. The Act, *inter alia*, deals with rights and obligations of depositories, depository participants, issuers and beneficial owners. A depository needs certificate from SEBI for commencement of business. Under the Act, SEBI has got powers to call for information and enquiry, give directions, levy penalties and adjudicate. Presently, there are two depositories, viz. National Securities Depository Ltd. and Central Depository Securities Ltd.

13.2.1 Depositories Act, 1996:

A. Objectives of the Act: The Act provides for the establishment of depositories in securities with the objective of ensuring free transferability of securities with speed, accuracy and security in the following manner:

1. Making securities of public limited companies freely transferable subject to certain exceptions.
2. Dematerialising the securities in the depository mode.
3. Providing for maintenance of ownership records in a book entry form.

In order to streamline the settlement process, the Act envisages the transfer of ownership of securities electronically by book entry without making the securities move from person to person. The Act has made the securities of all public limited companies freely transferable, restricting the company's right to use discretion in effecting the transfer of securities, and the transfer deed and other procedural requirements under the Companies Act have been dispensed with.

B. Benefits to Investors: These are as under:

1. **Speedy Transfer of Shares:** With the development of National Stock Exchange and the linking up of regional stock exchanges across the country purchase and sale of securities can be conveniently conducted between persons situated far away from each other.
2. **Avoidance of Trading Risks:** Depository system take care of large number of risks involved in traditional trading involving physical transfer of shares.
3. **Dematerialisation and Rematerialisation:** An investor holding share certificate can get it converted into electronic holding. Again if at some future date the investor wants to convert his electronic holding into share certificate, he is allowed such conversion which is called rematerialisation.

4. **Indemnification of Certain Losses:** Interest of owner of securities under depository mode is protected as the depository takes the responsibility of indemnifying owner for any loss caused due to negligence of the depository or depository participants.
5. **Low Brokerage Cost:** Brokerage cost in the case of dematerialisation is much lower than the cost as regards physical transfer of shares.

C. Right and Obligations of Depositories, Participants, Issuers and Beneficial Owners: These are as follows:

1. Agreement between Depository and Participants: A depository shall enter into an agreement with participant as its agent.
2. Services of Depository: Any person, through a participant, may enter into an agreement, in such form as may be specified by the by-laws, with any depository for availing its services.
3. Registration of Transfer of Services with Depository: Every depository shall, on receipt of intimate from a participant, registrar the transfer of security in the name of the transferee. If a beneficial owner or a transferee of any security seeks to have custody of such security, the depository shall inform the issuer accordingly.
4. Options to Receive Security Certificate or Hold Securities with Depository: Every person subscribing to securities offered by an issuer shall have the option either to receive the security certificates or hold securities with a depository. Where a person opts to hold a security with a depository, the issuer shall intimate such depository the details of allotment of the security, and on receipt of such information the depository shall enter in its records the name of the allottee as the beneficial owner of that security.
5. Securities in Depositories to be in Fungible Form: All securities held by a depository shall be dematerialized and shall be in a fungible form.
6. Rights of Depositories and Beneficial Owner: Notwithstanding

anything contained in any other law for the time being in force, a depository shall be deemed to be the registered owner for the purposes of effecting transfer of ownership of security on behalf of a beneficial owner. The depository as a registered owner shall not have any voting rights or any other rights in respect of securities held by it. The beneficial owner shall be entitled to all rights and benefits and be subjected to all the liabilities in respect of his securities held by a depository.

D. Other Provisions of the Act: These are as under:

1. A stock broker, in his dealings with the clients and the general investing public, must faithfully execute the orders for buying and selling of securities at the best available market price and not refuse to deal with a small investor merely on the ground of the volume of business involved.
2. A stock broker has to issue, without delay to his client, a contract note for all transactions in the specified form.
3. A stock broker must not disclose or discuss with any other person information of a confidential nature of the client which he comes to know in this business relationship.
4. A stock broker must not encourage sales or purchase of securities with the objective of generating brokerage or commission.
5. A stock broker should not deal or transact business knowingly, directly or indirectly, or execute an order for a client who has failed to carry out his commitments in relation to securities with another stock broker.
6. A stock broker who deals with a client must disclose whether he is acting as a principal or as an agent. He must ensure at the same time that no conflict of interest arises between him and the client.
7. A stock broker should have adequate trained staff and arrangements to render fair, prompt and competent services to the clients.

13.2.2 Securities and Exchange Board of India (Depositories and Participants) Regulations, 2018: SEBI notified the Securities and Exchange Board of India (Depositories and Participants) Regulations, 2018 on October 3, 2018 which gained immediate effect. The Securities and Exchange Board of India (Depositories and Participants) Regulations, 1996 (Old Regulation) stood repealed upon commencement of the new regulations.

A. Highlights of the New Regulation: These are as under:

1. Depositories to declare specific type of securities eligible for dematerialization.
2. Issuers to enter into agreements with depositories to enable the investors to dematerialize securities held by them.
3. There shall be continuous communication between the depositories, participants, issuers, issuers' agents.
4. A mechanism to be developed by depositories for protection of interest of the investors.
5. The interests of the beneficial owners against risks are to be protected by the depositories by applying adequate measures or through insurance.
6. There shall be co-operation between the depositories and the beneficial owners, issuers, issuer's agent, custodians of securities, clearing organizations for having an effective, prompt and accurate clearance and settlement of securities.
7. Participants to execute an agreement with beneficial owners as per the specified manner by the depositories before acting as a participant on his behalf.
8. Every beneficial owner is entitled to have statement of accounts from the participants as per the specified format as may be agreed between them.
9. Participants to submit periodic returns to the SEBI and their respective depositories as per the format specified by SEBI.
10. Participants to ensure safety and security of records and data submitted to them by the investors, issuers etc.
11. Issuers whose securities are eligible for dematerialization to have agreements with the depositories.
12. Depositories to establish an Investor Protection Fund.

13. The procedure of dematerialization of eligible securities has been established under the New Regulation.
14. Issuers or its agents to reconcile the records of dematerialized shares.
15. SEBI has the power to appoint an auditor to inspect or investigate, into the books of account, records, documents, infrastructures, systems and procedures or affairs of a depository, a participant, a beneficial owner, an issuer or its agent.
16. SEBI has the absolute authority to take any action against any issuer or its agent, whoever contravenes any provisions of the New Regulation.

13.3 Companies Act, 2013: Main Provisions

The Companies Act, 1956 was in need of a substantial revamp for quite some time, to make it more contemporary and relevant to corporates, regulators and other stakeholders in India. Therefore, it was replaced by Companies Act, 2013.

13.3.1 Types of Companies:

1. **One-person Company:** The 2013 Act introduces a new type of entity to the existing list i.e. apart from forming a public or private limited company, the 2013 Act enables the formation of a new entity a 'one-person company' (OPC). An OPC means a company with only one person as its member [Section 3(1) of 2013 Act].
2. **Private Company:** The 2013 Act introduces a change in the definition for a private company, *inter alia*, the new requirement increases the limit of the number of members from 50 to 200 [Section 2(68) of 2013 Act].
3. **Small Company:** A small company has been defined as a company, other than a public company.

- Paid-up share capital of which does not exceed ` 50 lakh or such higher amount as may be prescribed which shall not be more than ` 5 crore.
- Turnover of which as per its last profit-and-loss account does not exceed ` 2 crore or such higher amount as may be

prescribed which shall not be more than ` 20 crore:

As set out in the 2013 Act, this section will not be applicable to the following: (a) a holding company or a subsidiary company, (b) a company registered under Section 8 and (c) a company or body corporate governed by any special Act [Section 2(85) of 2013 Act].

4. **Dormant Company:** The 2013 Act states that a company can be classified as dormant when it is formed and registered under this 2013 Act for a future project or to hold an asset or intellectual property and has no significant accounting transaction. Such a company or an inactive one may apply to the ROC in such manner as may be prescribed for obtaining the status of a dormant company [Section 455 of 2013 Act].

13.3.2 Mergers and Acquisitions: The 2013 Act features some new provisions in the area of mergers and acquisitions, apart from making certain changes from the existing provisions. While the changes are aimed at simplifying and rationalising the procedures involved, the new provisions are also aimed at ensuring higher accountability for the company and majority shareholders and increasing flexibility for corporates. The 2013 Act has streamlined as well as introduced concepts such as reverse mergers (merger of foreign companies with Indian companies) and squeeze-out provisions, which are significant. The 2013 Act has also introduced the requirement for valuations in several cases, including mergers and acquisitions, by registered valuers.

13.3.3 Prohibition of Association or Partnership of Persons Exceeding Certain Number: The 2013 Act puts a restriction on the number of partners that can be admitted to a partnership at 100. To be specific, the 2013 Act states that no association or partnership consisting of more than the given number of persons as may be prescribed shall be formed for the purpose of carrying on any business that has for its object the acquisition of gain by the association or partnership or by the individual members thereof, unless it is registered as a company under this 1956 Act or is formed under any other law for the time being in force.

As an exception, the aforesaid restriction would not apply to the following: (a) A Hindu undivided family carrying on any business and (b) an association or partnership, if it is formed by professionals who are governed by special acts like the Chartered Accountants Act etc. [Section 464 of 2013 Act].

13.3.4 Insider Trading and Prohibition on Forward Dealings: The 2013 Act for the first time defines insider trading and price-sensitive information and prohibits any person including the director or key managerial person from entering into insider trading [Section 195 of 2013 Act]. Further, the Act also prohibits directors and key managerial personnel from forward dealings in the company or its holding, subsidiary or associate company [Section 194 of 2013 Act].

13.3.5 Corporate Governance: The 2013 Act intends to improve corporate governance by requiring disclosure of nature of concern or interest of every director, manager, any other key managerial personnel and relatives of such a director, manager or any other key managerial personnel and reduction in threshold of disclosure from 20 percent to 2 percent. The term 'key managerial personnel' has now been defined in the 2013 Act and means the chief executive officer, managing director, manager, company secretary, whole-time director, chief financial officer and any such other officer as may be prescribed.

13.3.6 Accounts and Audit: The 2013 Act has introduced certain significant amendments in this chapter. It has also introduced several additional requirements such as preparation of consolidated financial statements, additional reporting requirements for the directors in their report such as the development and implementation of the risk management policy, disclosures in respect of voting rights not exercised directly by the employees in respect of shares to which the scheme relates, etc., in comparison with the requirements of the 1956 Act.

The 2013 Act features extensive changes within the area of audit and auditors with a view to enhance audit effectiveness and accountability of the auditors. These changes undoubtedly, have a considerable impact on the audit profession. However, it needs to be noted that these changes will also have a considerable impact on the company in terms of time, efforts and expectations involved. Apart from introducing new concepts such as rotation of audit firms and class action suits, the 2013 Act also increases the auditor's liability substantially in comparison with the 1956 Act.

Unlike the appointment process at each annual general meeting under the 1956 Act, the auditor will now be appointed for a period of 5 years, with a requirement to ratify such an appointment at each annual general meeting [Section 139(1) of 2013 Act].

13.3.7 Dividend: The 2013 Act proposes to introduce significant changes to the existing provisions of the 1956 Act in respect of declaration of dividend. The changes are likely to affect the existing practices followed by companies with regard to the declaration of dividend.

The existing provisions of the 1956 Act in relation to the transfer of a specified percentage of profit to reserve is no longer applicable and thus, companies will be free to transfer any or no amount to its reserves.

13.3.8 Revival and Rehabilitation of Sick Companies: Chapter XIX of the 2013 Act lays down the provisions for the revival and rehabilitation of sick companies. The chapter describes the circumstances which determine the declaration of a company as a sick company, and also includes the rehabilitation process of the same. Although it aims to provide comprehensive provisions for the revival and rehabilitation of sick companies, the fact that several provisions such as particulars, documents as well as content of the draft scheme in respect of application for revival and rehabilitation, etc. have been left to substantive enactment, leaves scope for interpretation.

The coverage of this chapter is no longer restricted to industrial companies, and the determination of the net worth would not be relevant for assessing whether a company is a sick company.

13.3.9 Corporate Social Responsibility: The 2013 Act makes an effort to introduce the culture of corporate social responsibility (CSR) in Indian corporates by requiring companies to formulate a corporate social responsibility policy and at least incur a given minimum expenditure on social activities.

13.4 Limited Liability Partnership (LLP) Act, 2008

LLP Act, 2008 provides for a flexible governance structure to be determined by the partners themselves by mutual agreement, easy compliance requirements in comparison to companies, combined with limitation of liability to the extent of the partner's contribution.

The salient features of the LLP Act, 2008 are as under:

1. LLP shall be a body corporate and a legal entity separate from its partners. It will have perpetual succession. Indian Partnership Act, 1932 shall not be applicable to LLPs, since LLP shall be in the form of a body corporate.
2. An LLP has to be incorporated with a minimum of two persons. The Act does not restrict the benefit of LLP structure to certain classes of professionals only and would be available for use by any enterprise which fulfils the requirements of the Act.
3. The LLP will be an alternative corporate business vehicle that would give the benefits of limited liability but would allow its members the flexibility of organizing their internal structure as a partnership based on an agreement.
4. On registration, LLP shall be capable of: (a) suing and being sued and (b) acquiring, owning, holding and developing or disposing off property.
5. A person may cease to be a partner of a LLP in accordance with an agreement with the other partners or in absence of agreement with the other partners, by giving a notice in

writing of not less than 30 days of his intention to resign as partner.

6. In the event of an act carried out by a LLP, or any of its partners, with intend to defraud creditors of the LLP or any other person or for any fraudulent purpose, the liability of the LLP and partners, who acted with intend to defraud creditors or for any fraudulent purpose shall be unlimited for all or any of the debts or other liabilities of the LLP.
7. A contribution of a partner may consist of tangible, movable or immovable or intangible property or other benefits to the LLP including money, promissory notes, other agreements to contribute cash or property, and contracts for services performed or to be performed.
8. While the LLP will be a separate legal entity, liable to the full extent of its assets, the liability of the partners would be limited to their agreed contribution in the LLP. Further, no partner would be liable on account of the independent or unauthorized actions of other partners, thus allowing individual partners to be shielded from joint liability created by another partner's wrongful business decisions or misconduct.
9. An LLP shall be under obligation to maintain annual accounts reflecting true and fair view of its state of affairs.
10. Provisions have been made in the Act for corporate actions like mergers, amalgamations etc.
11. There is a provision of voluntary winding up as well as winding up by the Tribunal.
12. There are provisions for inter conversion of LLP into private company etc.

LLP Act should pave the way for greater corporatisation of the small and medium enterprises, thereby enhancing their access to equity and funds from the market.

13.5 Insolvency and Bankruptcy Code (IBC), 2016

There can be many reasons why an enterprise needs to close down—voluntary or forced by circumstances. The ease of closing down business is crucial for a good entrepreneurship ecosystem.

13.5.1 Need for Entrepreneur-friendly Bankruptcy Laws: With globalisation and competition, the possibility of a large number of manufacturing enterprises not getting business, and having to close, has to be particularly catered to. The experimental character of entrepreneurship and the risks involved need to be understood so that an entrepreneur gets another chance in which he/she may do better. The business environment can be strengthened by reducing the bankruptcy stigma and facilitating re-starts. Unfortunately, a great deal of emphasis is placed on stigmatizing failure. The underlying message is that if an entrepreneur has failed once, he would not be given a second chance. A policy change is needed here. Unless there has been wilful default, surreptitious draining of resources etc., a failed entrepreneur may have actually learnt from his mistakes and become a good investment bet.

At a broader level, the bankruptcy laws should be designed to help viable companies in distress, and make closing and re-starting easier. Enterprises need insolvency procedures which recognise that viable businesses can suffer from temporary problems, e.g. an economy-wide recession. Such procedures should facilitate the necessary internal reorganisation and restructuring of debt. A key objective of the bankruptcy laws should be to help viable companies survive while safeguarding the interests of the creditors. This requires being able to distinguish quickly and at low cost between firms to restructure and firms to close.

The policies and institutions of an economy should provide adequate freedom to every person to enable him to pursue his economic interests meaningfully. Inclusive economies provide such freedom to pursue vocation, create a level playing field for good ideas to replace obsolete ones, and encourage scarce resources to pursue the most productive avenues. Such economies unleash and realize full potential of every person and thereby develop faster.

Business plans entail informed risk taking to compete and succeed. Either incumbents are displaced by new businesses or new businesses fail to carve out a competitive space for themselves. Either way, failure of some businesses is integral to a market economy. When a business fails, it needs to be resolved at the earliest and expeditiously.

Any undue delay in commencement or conclusion of resolution may lead to exodus of key stakeholders and aggravate the failure, sometimes beyond repair. If the resolution is not possible, an orderly exit mechanism should allow stakeholders to recover their dues from liquidation proceeds of the business and free-up resources for reallocation.

In many countries reforms have taken place that allow insolvency of businesses to be dealt with in a comprehensive manner that enables revival or rescue before liquidation and winding up. Insolvency is treated as a commercial phenomenon requiring to be dealt with in accordance with commercial principles in a framework of fairness and equity. There is an independent institutionalized process of providing a grace period for businesses to deal with distress. This is intended to enable a revival plan if the business is inherently viable, puts all creditors on hold pending revival, gets business out of holding period if it revives or takes action on winding up if the business is non-revivable. Both personal as well as business insolvency are dealt with on the basis of similar principles with ease of filing for bankruptcy and securing of certain protection from creditor action once this is done.

13.5.2 Situation Prior to IBC, 2016: Unlike limited liability entities, where the liability of the shareholder is limited to the extent of the contribution made or due from him, in proprietorships or partnerships there is no separation of personal and business liability. When a business fails, not only do the assets of the business but the entrepreneur's personal assets also get attached to pay off business dues. Further, all guarantors of the small entrepreneur get personally involved and in the eventuality of failure they also get implicated.

Prior to the implementation of IBC, 2016, insolvency of business entities was governed by a host of outdated legislations. The focus in these laws was not revival followed by structured exit in case of failure, but on recovery of outstanding dues through a court-driven process. The relevant courts under the statutes were district courts which took their own time adjudicating the petitions and were apt to enforce the processes of seizing debtor's estates, appointing receivers and punitive remedies against the debtor including imprisonment rather than enabling any revival or turnaround. Indeed adjudicatory order on an insolvency petition under these statutes laid the entrepreneur open to action including arrest and detention in a civil prison as if business failure was a criminal act.

The existing legal framework for insolvency and bankruptcy was spread across multiple statutes and was found to be inadequate resulting in undue delays in resolution and thus rendering it ineffective, at times. In an economy growing at a rapid pace not only the credit delivery mechanism but also the economic culture surrounding it needs to be as per best global practice. Thus there was need for an effective statutory framework to deal with insolvency and bankruptcy to facilitate development of credit markets in the country, encourage entrepreneurship, improving ease of doing business, facilitate investments, create more employment opportunities leading to higher economic growth and development.

A closure of an enterprise required, *inter alia*, legal compliances related to labour laws, taxation laws, power utility, water utility, municipal body, creditors, financial institutions etc. Even when the laws were clear enough on the requirements to be fulfilled, the implementation of the same was problematic for micro, small and medium enterprise (MSMEs).

There was no mechanism that rescued failed firms or released resources from failed firms to alternate firms. The resources did not move seamlessly from less competitive firms to more competitive firms continuously. This deterred optimal utilization of resources and dampened entrepreneurship.

The promoters stayed in control of the company even after default. The creditors were ineffectual in recovering their dues.

There was, thus, a need to streamline the procedures, reduce discretion and intermediation.

13.5.3 Bankruptcy Law Reforms Committee (BLRC): BLRC (Chairman: T.K. Viswanathan) was set up on August 22, 2014 for providing an entrepreneur-friendly legal bankruptcy framework, as announced in the Budget Speech of the Finance Minister for the year 2014-15. BLRC submitted its Report and Draft Bill to the Finance Minister on November 4, 2015. Based on this, a Draft Bill, namely The Insolvency and Bankruptcy Code, 2015 was introduced in the Lok Sabha on December 21, 2015.

13.5.4 Insolvency and Bankruptcy Code (IBC), 2016: IBC, 2016 is the bankruptcy law of India which consolidated the existing framework by creating a single law for insolvency and bankruptcy.

IBC, 2016 is a one-stop solution for resolving insolvencies. A strong insolvency framework—where the cost and time incurred are minimal in attaining liquidation—was long overdue in India. IBC, 2016 is intended to protect the interests of small investors and make the process of doing business a less cumbersome process.

Insolvency and Bankruptcy Code, 2015 was introduced in the Lok Sabha on December 21, 2015 by Finance Minister Shri Arun Jaitley. It was referred to a Joint Committee of Parliament on December 23, 2015, which recommended it on April 28, 2016. The Code was passed by the Lok Sabha on May 5, 2016 and by the Rajya Sabha on May 11, 2016.

The Code received assent from President Shri Pranab Mukherjee on May 28, 2016 and was notified in The Gazette of India on May 28, 2016. It became effective in December 2016.

It repealed the Presidency Towns Insolvency Act, 1909 and Sick Industrial Companies (Special Provisions) Repeal Act, 2003, among others.

A. Key Features: These are as under:

1. **Insolvency Resolution**: IBC, 2016 outlines separate insolvency resolution processes for individuals, companies and partnership firms. The process may be initiated by either the debtor or the creditors. A maximum time limit, for completion of the insolvency resolution process, has been set for corporates and individuals. For companies, the process will have to be completed in 180 days, which may be extended by 90 days, if a majority of the creditors agree. For start-ups (other than partnership firms), small companies and other companies (with assets less than ` 1 crore), resolution process would be completed within 90 days of initiation of request which may be extended by 45 days.
2. **Insolvency Regulator**: Insolvency and Bankruptcy Board of India (IBBI) has been established under IBC, 2016 to oversee the insolvency proceedings in the country and regulate the entities registered under it. IBBI will have 10 members, including representatives from the Ministries of Finance and Law, and the Reserve Bank of India.
3. **Insolvency Professionals**: The insolvency process will be managed by licensed professionals. These professionals will also control the assets of the debtor during the insolvency process.
4. **Bankruptcy and Insolvency Adjudicator**: IBC, 2016 proposes two separate tribunals to oversee the process of insolvency resolution, for individuals and companies: (a) National Company Law Tribunal for companies and limited liability partnership firms and (b) Debt Recovery Tribunal for individuals and partnerships.
5. **Procedure:** A plea for insolvency is submitted to the adjudicating authority (NCLT in case of corporate debtors) by financial or operation creditors or the corporate debtor itself. The maximum time allowed to either accept or reject the plea is 14 days. If the plea is accepted, the tribunal has to appoint an insolvency resolution professional (IRP) to draft a resolution plan within 180 days (extendable by 90 days),

following which the corporate insolvency resolution process (CIRP) is initiated by the court. For the said period, the board of directors of the company stands suspended, and the promoters do not have a say in the management of the company. The IRP, if required, can seek the support of the company's management for day-to-day operations. If the CIRP fails in reviving the company the liquidation process is initiated.

13.5.5 Amendments: IBC, 2016 was amended in 2017 to prohibit certain persons from submitting a resolution plan in case of defaults, and to prohibit the sale of property of a defaulter to such persons during liquidation.

13.5.6 Insolvency and Bankruptcy Board of India (IBBI): IBBI was set up on October 1, 2016 under the Insolvency and Bankruptcy Code, 2016. It has regulatory oversight over the insolvency professionals, insolvency professional agencies and information utilities. It writes and enforces rules for transactions, namely corporate insolvency resolution, corporate liquidation, individual insolvency resolution and individual bankruptcy under IBC, 2016. It is a key pillar of the ecosystem responsible for implementation of IBC, 2016.

In short, IBC, 2016 consolidates and amends the laws relating to reorganization and insolvency resolution of corporate persons, partnership firms and individuals in a time bound manner for maximization of the value of assets of such persons, to promote entrepreneurship, availability of credit and balance the interests of all the stakeholders.

IBC, 2016 enables a firm to get in and get out of business with ease, keep striving for resurrection and new pursuits, undeterred by honest business failures. It reduces incidence of failure in two ways. First, the inevitable consequence of default in terms of insolvency proceedings prompts behavioural changes on the part of debtor to try hard to prevent business failure. Second, it reduces failure by setting in motion a process that rehabilitates failing but viable businesses. If rehabilitation is not possible, IBC, 2016 facilitates closure of businesses with the least cost and disruptions. It thus addresses business failures by reducing the chances of failure, rescuing failing businesses where possible and releasing resources from businesses, where rehabilitation is not possible and thereby promotes entrepreneurship. It improves availability of credit by: (a) preventing default, (b) recovering default from future earnings of the firm, post resolution and (c) recovering default from sale of liquidation assets.

It enables the optimum utilization of resources, all the time, either by: (a) preventing use of resources below the optimum potential, (b) ensuring efficient resource use within the firm through resolution of insolvency or (c) releasing unutilized or under-utilized resources for efficient uses through closure of the firm.

By liberating the resources stuck up in inefficient and defunct firms for continuous recycling, the IBC, 2016, has completed the circle of freedom to enter, started by economic reforms since 1991, with freedom to exit.

14

Foreign Portfolio Investment in Indian Stock Market

The wave of liberalisation and globalisation sweeping across the world has opened many national markets for international business. Global private investment, in most part, is now made by multinational corporations (MNCs) also referred to as transnational corporations (TNCs). Clearly, these transnational organisations play a major role in world trade and investments because of their demonstrated management skills, technology, financial resources and related advantages. Recent developments in the global market are indicative of the rapidly growing international business. The beginning of the 21st century has already marked a tremendous growth of international investments, trade and financial transactions along with the integration and openness of international markets.

Foreign investment is a subject of topical interest. Countries of the world, particularly developing economies, are vying with each other to attract foreign capital to boost their domestic rates of investment and also to acquire new technology and managerial skills. Intense competition is taking place among the fund-starved less developed countries to lure foreign investors by offering repatriation facilities, tax concessions and other incentives. However, foreign investment is not an unmixed blessing. Governments in developing countries have to be very careful while deciding the magnitude, pattern and conditions of private foreign investment.

14.1 Foreign Investment: New Strategy for Faster Growth

Recent years have witnessed a dramatic world-wide increase in foreign investment, accompanied by a marked change in the attitude of most developing countries towards inward foreign investment. As against a highly suspicious attitude of these countries towards foreign investment in the past, most countries now regard it as beneficial for their development efforts and compete with each other to attract it. The explanation for this shift in attitude lies in the changes in political and economic systems that have occurred during the closing years of the 20th century. Many countries, particularly in Eastern Europe, have abandoned socialism in its various forms and embraced the market economy. In many of these countries, mass privatisation has taken place mainly with funds from abroad. The success of East Asian economies is attributable chiefly to a high level of foreign investment and export promotion.

Foreign investment is a zero-sum game in which a country can attract investment only at the expense of another country. Additional investment is likely to take place when new investment opportunities emerge in countries opening up to the world. All countries have the chance to become attractive to foreign investors, not only large and advanced countries.

In the 1980s, foreign investment was concentrated within the Triad (EU, Japan and the USA). However, in the 1990s, investment flows to developed countries declined while those to developing countries increased in response to rapid economic growth and fewer restrictions. The global trends in investment and the attitude of the developing world towards it have shown marked changes over the last few decades.

During the period 1950-1980, developing countries of the world relied on restricting imports, promoting exports and adopting import substitution along with pegged exchange rate regime. They relied heavily on debt and grants for external capital. The countries which followed these policies faced structural balance of payments problem and consequently had to open their economies by inviting foreign investments and liberalising their trade regime. Over the recent past, there has been a marked change in the relative significance of foreign investments vis-à-vis debt and grants.

The growth of investment flows to developing countries is unevenly distributed among regions and groups of developing countries. Most investment flows continue to be concentrated overwhelmingly in Asia and Latin America. China is now the largest host country in the developing world. However, countries with poor infrastructure, high indebtedness, slow progress in market-oriented reforms and low technological capabilities are not attractive to foreign investors. The rapid increase in foreign investment has been accompanied by significant changes in the sectoral composition, from the primary sector and resource-based manufacturing towards services and technology-intensive industries. Figure 14.1 shows factors which affect foreign portfolio investment in a country.

14.2 Portfolio versus Direct Investment

There are two main types of foreign investments: portfolio investments and direct investments. Portfolio investments are purely financial assets, such as bonds, denominated in a national currency. With bonds, the investor simply lends capital to get fixed payouts or a return at regular intervals and then receives the face value of the bond at a pre-specified date. Portfolio or financial investments take place primarily through financial institutions such as banks and investment funds.

Direct investments, on the other hand, are real investments in factories, capital goods, land, and inventories where both capital and management are involved and the investor retains control over use of the invested capital. Direct investment usually takes the form of a firm starting a subsidiary or taking control of another firm (for example, by purchasing a majority of the stock).

In the international context, direct investments are usually undertaken by multinational corporations engaged in manufacturing, resource extraction, or services. Direct investments are now as important as portfolio investments as forms or channels of international private capital flows.

Figure 14.1: Factors Affecting Foreign Portfolio Inflows in India

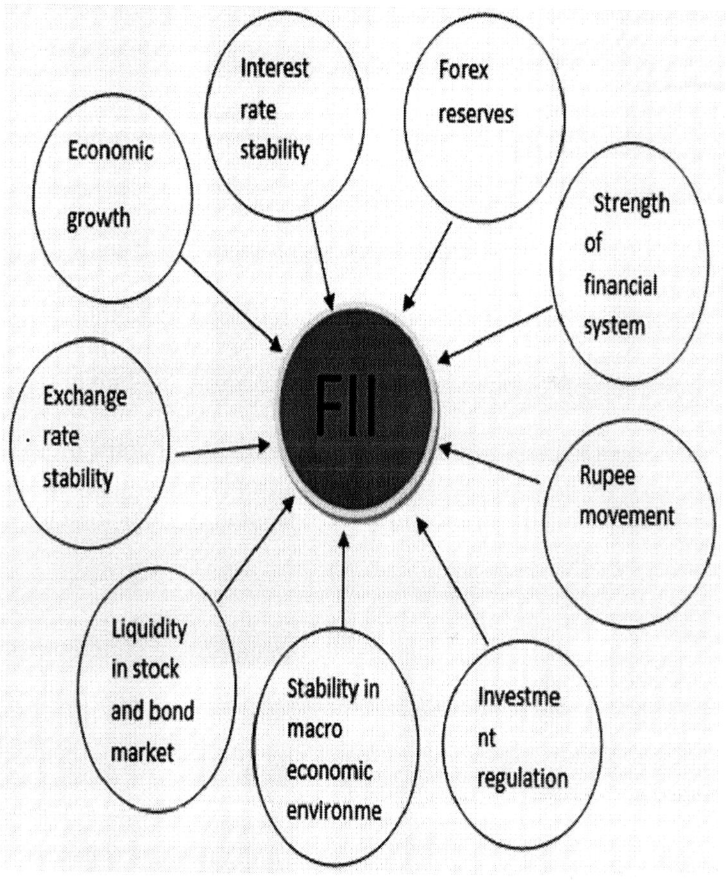

14.3 Foreign Institutional Investors (FIIs)

The basic motive for international portfolio investments is to earn higher returns abroad. Thus, residents of one country purchase bonds of another country if the returns on bonds are higher in the other country. This is the simple and straight forward outcome of yield maximization and tends to equalize returns internationally.

Institutional investors are specialised financial intermediaries managing savings collectively on behalf of investors, especially small investors, towards specific objectives in terms of risk, returns, and maturity of claims. Portfolio investors provide institutional character to the capital markets, flavoured by highly intensive research and diversified investments. Foreign institutional investors (FIIs) inject global liquidity into the markets, raise the price-earning ratio and thus reduce the cost of capital. From the perspective of FIIs, investments in various countries provide a measure of portfolio diversification and hedging as also to take advantage of arbitrage opportunities.

FIIs make investments in various countries to provide a measure of portfolio diversification and hedging to their assets. The forces driving the recent change in the investment portfolio of FIIs, as reflected in the growing emphasis on equities of emerging market economies, include *inter alia*: (a) increased accessibility of these markets after liberalisation, (b) improved marketability, (c) fewer problems relating to thin trading and (d) improved macroeconomic fundamentals of these countries.

14.4 Advantages of Portfolio Investment Inflows

Following are the chief advantages of having portfolio investments by foreigners.

14.4.1 Improvement in Corporate Capital Structure: FIIs are well-known for a greater appetite for equity than debt in their asset structure. Thus, opening up the economy to FIIs is in line with the accepted preference for non-debt creating foreign inflows over foreign debt. Furthermore, because of this preference for equities over bonds, portfolio inflows can help in compressing the yield-differential between equity and bonds and improve corporate capital structure.

14.4.2 Competition in Financial Markets: Institutional investors promote financial innovation and development of hedging instruments. Institutions, for example, because of their interest in hedging risks, are known to have contributed to the development of zero-coupon bonds and index futures. FIIs, as professional bodies of asset managers and financial analysts, not only enhance competition in financial markets, but also improve the alignment of asset prices to fundamentals.

Institutions in general and FIIs in particular are known to have good information and low transaction costs. By aligning asset prices closer to fundamentals, they stabilize markets. Fundamentals are known to be sluggish in their movements. Thus, if prices are aligned to fundamentals, they should be as stable as the fundamentals themselves. Furthermore, FIIs with a variety of risk-return preferences also help in dampening volatility.

14.4.3 Enhanced Efficiency in Capital Markets: FIIs as professional bodies of asset managers and financial analysts enhance competition and efficiency of financial markets. Equity market development aids economic development. By increasing the availability of riskier long-term capital for projects, FIIs can help in the process of economic development.

14.4.4 Improvement in Corporate Governance: Good corporate governance is essential to overcome the principal-agent problem between shareholders and management. Information asymmetries and incomplete contracts between share-holders and management are at the root of the agency costs. Bad corporate governance makes equity finance a costly option.

FIIs contribute to better understanding of operations and improve corporate governance of firms. Institutions are known for challenging excessive executive compensation, and removing under performing managers. There is some evidence that institutionalization increases dividend payouts, and enhances productivity growth.

14.5 Disadvantages of Portfolio Investment Inflows

Among others, the two common apprehensions about FIIs inflows are the fear of management takeovers and potential capital outflows.

14.5.1 Management Control: FIIs act as agents on behalf

of their principals as financial investors maximising returns. There are domestic laws that effectively prohibit institutional investors from taking management control. For example, in India, all takeovers are governed by Substantial Acquisition of Shares and Takeovers Regulations, 1997, framed by Securities and Exchange Board of India (SEBI). In the absence of such laws, management takeover by foreigners is possible.

14.5.2 Volatility of Portfolio Flows: FIIs inflows are popularly described as *hot money* because of the herd behaviour and potential for large capital outflows. Herd behaviour means FIIs trying to either only buy or only sell at the same time, particularly at times of market stress. Value at risk models followed by FIIs may destabilise markets by leading to simultaneous sale by various FIIs. Extrapolative expectations or trend chasing, rather than focusing on fundamentals, can lead to destabilization.

It has been argued that under the process of globalisation, highly diversified investors participate in cross-border movement of capital. Such investors pay little attention to economic fundamentals and in the presence of asymmetric information they resort to herd behaviour, which results in volatility of international capital flows. Such a view has, however, been challenged and it has been argued that there is high level of substitutability between various forms of foreign capital.

Countries with modest growth potentials and semi-developed financial market infrastructure are most vulnerable to reversal of portfolio investment flows. Existence of large asymmetry of information in such countries can lead to sharp changes in portfolio and private debt flows in the face of even a slight change in investor perception about the health of the recipient economy. This type of volatility is, however, not limited to portfolio flows. Even external commercial borrowings, in the form of bank borrowing or bond financing, show similar patterns.

14.5.3 Pro-cyclical: The most important disadvantage of portfolio inflows is that it tends to be pro-cyclical, in the sense that it comes in when the balance of payments (BOP) position is seen to be strong and goes out when the BOP position is expected to weaken. Thus, it accentuates the direction of movement of the BOP, which can cause serious problems in macroeconomic management. In the case of countries where the foreign exchange markets are very thin as compared to the international financial market, a free FII regime carries the danger of speculative movements, which can lead to serious disruption in the economy.

14.5.4 Hedge Funds: Hedge funds are another source of concern which (unlike pension funds, life insurance companies and mutual funds) engage in short-term trading, take short positions and borrow more aggressively.

There are also downside risks of portfolio inflows. The downside risks include political risk, currency risk, problems associated with low liquidity and volatility on returns. Cross-country studies indicate that reversal of portfolio flows could be disorderly and result in substantial economic hardship for developing countries.

14.5.5 Foreign Portfolio Investors are Fair-weather Friends: In rapidly growing economies, high real gross domestic product (GDP) growth needs concomitant growth in monetary aggregates, which also needs expansion of base money. To this extent, the accretion of foreign exchange reserves to the central bank's balance sheet is helpful in expanding base money at the required rate. However, net capital flows and accretion to foreign exchange reserves in excess of such requirements necessitate sterilisation and more active monetary and macroeconomic management. Thus, large inflows of capital, well in excess of the current financing needs, can lead to high domestic credit and monetary growth, boom in stock market and other asset prices, leading to macroeconomic and financial instability. Abrupt reversals in capital flows also lead to significant difficulties in monetary and macroeconomic management.

Reversals of capital flows are quick, necessitating a painful adjustment in bank credit, and collapse of stock prices. Such reversals also result in the contraction of the central bank's balance sheet, which may be difficult to compensate with accretion of domestic assets as fast as the reserves depletion. These developments can then lead to banking and currency crises, large employment and output losses and huge fiscal costs. Thus, the boom and bust pattern of capital inflows can, unless managed proactively, result in macroeconomic and financial instability. Hence, the monetary authorities in developing countries need to watch closely and continuously financial and economic developments in the advanced economies and also manage their capital account actively.

14.6 Liberalisation of Portfolio Investment Flows into India

Prior to 1992, only non-resident Indians (NRIs) and overseas corporate bodies (OCBs) were allowed to undertake portfolio investment in India. In line with the recommendations of the High Level Committee on Balance of Payments (Chairman: C. Rangarajan), FIIs were allowed to invest in the Indian debt and equity market. FII investments first started flowing into India in 1993. Portfolio investment inflows have since then been substantial.

14.6.1 Investments by FIIs: India embarked on a gradual shift towards capital account convertibility with the launch of the reforms in the early 1990s. Although foreign natural persons—except NRIs—are prohibited from investing in financial assets, such investments are permitted by FIIs and Overseas Corporate Bodies (OCBs) with suitable restrictions. From September 14, 1992, FIIs were allowed to invest in all the securities traded on the primary and secondary markets, including shares, debentures and warrants issued by companies which were listed or were to be listed on the stock exchanges in India and in the schemes floated by domestic mutual funds. Funds invested by FIIs must have at least 50 participants with no one holding more than 5 percent to ensure a broad base and preventing such investment acting as a camouflage for individual investment in the nature of FDI and requiring Government approval.

The idea of allowing FIIs was that they were broad-based, diversified funds, leaving out individual foreign investors and foreign companies. The only exceptions were the NRI and OCB portfolio investments through the secondary market, which were subject to individual ceilings of 5 percent to prevent a possible *takeover*. Individuals were left out because of the difficulties in checking on their antecedents, and of their lack of expertise in market matters and relatively short-term perspective. OCB investments through the portfolio route were banned in November 2001.

During 1992-93, Government allowed reputed FIIs including pension funds, mutual funds, asset management companies, investment trusts nominee companies and incorporated or institutional portfolio managers to invest in the Indian capital market subject to the condition that they registered with the Securities and Exchange Board of India (SEBI) and obtained RBI approval under FERA.

In 1996-97, the guidelines for investment by FIIs were further liberalised. The limit of investment for an individual FII was raised from 5 percent to 10 percent subject, however, to the aggregate limit of 24 percent for all FIIs. The FIIs were also allowed to invest in unlisted companies in the same manner as they were allowed to invest in listed companies. FII investments in debt securities of companies as 100 percent debt funds were allowed subject to certain guidelines. FIIs were also allowed to invest in the gilt-edged government securities with the framework of guidelines. FIIs were also allowed to invest in the gilt-edged government securities within the framework of guidelines, and proprietary funds have been allowed to invest in the country through the FII route.

As a follow up of the announcement made in the Union Budget 1997-98, aggregate investment ceilings for FIIs and Non-resident Indians (including OCBs) were increased up to 30 percent subject to approval by the company's shareholders.

Guidelines for foreign investment in preference shares issued by the Indian companies were also issued. These provided greater flexibility to Indian corporations in using preference shares as a form of financing. FIIs were also permitted to purchase/sell Treasury Bills within the overall approved debt ceilings.

A number of liberalization measures were taken in 1998-99 to promote portfolio foreign investment. In order to avoid NRIs being crowded out by FIIs, the aggregate ceiling for investment in a company by all NRIs/PIOs/OCBs through stock exchanges was made separate and exclusive of the investment ceiling available for FIIs. In addition, the aggregate investment ceiling for NRIs/PIOs/OCBs was raised from 5 percent to 10 percent of the paid-up capital of a company. In the case of listed Indian companies, the ceiling was raised to 24 percent of the paid-up capital under a General Body Resolution. Also, the investment limit by a single NRI/PIO/OCB was enhanced from 1 percent to 5 percent of the paid up capital. Policy pertaining to investment in unlisted companies was liberalised. NRIs/PIOs/OCBs were permitted to invest in unlisted companies.

FIIs were allowed to purchase and sell Government securities and treasury bills within overall approved debt ceilings. To facilitate better risk management by investors, authorised dealers were permitted to provide forward cover to FIIs in respect of their fresh equity investments in India. Moreover, transactions among FIIs with respect to Indian stocks were no longer required post-facto conformation from the RBI. Also, 100 percent FII debt funds were permitted to invest in unlisted debt securities of Indian companies.

In March 1999, the RBI issued a notification granting general permission to mutual funds for issuing units to NRIs/PIOs/OCBs subject to certain specified norms, thereby dispensing with the existing procedure of obtaining prior permission. In addition, approval procedures were simplified by the RBI in respect of NRIs/PIOs/OCBs by granting them general permission in lieu of case by case approval procedure in a large number of areas. This included acceptance of deposits by Indian companies, investment in air taxi operations, sale of shares in stock exchanges, transfer of shares in stock exchanges, transfer of share/bonds/debentures and immovable properly to charitable trusts/organisations in India as gift, raising of loans by resident individuals/proprietorship concerns on non-repatriable basis, issue of commercial papers by Indian companies to NRIs etc.

In 1999-2000, with a view to expand the FIIs category, the Government permitted foreign corporates and high net worth individuals to invest through SEBI registered FIIs. Such investments were subject to a sub-limit of 5 percent within the aggregate limit for FII portfolio investments of 24 percent in a single company. Government also permitted SEBI registered domestic fund managers to manage foreign funds for investment in the Indian capital market through the portfolio investment route provided the funds were channelled through internationally recognised financial institutions and subject to the reporting requirements as applicable to FIIs.

In 2000-01, FIIs were permitted greater leverage in the primary/secondary markets by allowing enhancement of the aggregate FII investment ceiling in the issued and paid-up capital of Indian companies from the normal ceiling of 24 percent to 40 percent subject to prescribed procedures. The list of activities of non-banking financial companies (NBFCs) eligible for foreign equity investment was increased to 18 with the addition of micro-credit/rural credit. Foreign investment guidelines for NBFCs were amended for providing a minimum capitalisation norm of US$ 0.5 million for activities, which were not fund-based or consultative in nature, irrespective of the foreign equity participation level. The provision applied to investment advisory services, credit reference and rating agencies, financial consultancy, foreign exchange broking and money changing. Permission was granted to holding companies in NBFC activities with minimum capital of US$ 5 million, subject to specific conditions of disinvestment.

In order to provide stimulus to the growth of the venture capital industry in India, SEBI was made the single point nodal agency for registration of both domestic and overseas venture capital funds. Venture capital companies/funds were allowed to invest through the automatic route, subject to SEBI regulations and sector specific caps on FDI.

In February 2000, the FII regulations were amended to permit foreign corporates and high net worth individuals to also invest as sub-accounts of SEBI-registered FIIs. Foreign corporates and high net worth individuals fall outside the category of diversified investors. FIIs were also permitted to seek SEBI registration in respect of sub-accounts for their clients under the regulations. [1]

While initially FIIs were permitted to manage the sub-account of clients, the domestic portfolio managers or domestic asset management companies were also allowed to manage the funds of such sub-accounts and also to make application on behalf of such sub-accounts. Such sub-accounts could be an institution, or a fund, or a portfolio established or incorporated outside India, or a broad-based fund, or a proprietary fund, or even a foreign corporate or individual. So, in practice there are common categories of entities, which could be registered as both FIIs and sub-accounts. However, investment into a sub-account is to be made either by FIIs, or by domestic portfolio manager or asset management company, and not by itself directly.

In view of the concerns of some unregulated entities taking positions in the stock market through the mechanism of participatory notes (PNs) issued by FIIs, the issue was examined by the Ministry of Finance in consultation with RBI and SEBI. Following these consultations, in January 2004, SEBI stipulated that PNs are not to be issued to any non-regulated entity, and the principle of *know your clients* may be strictly adhered to. SEBI has indicated that the existing non-eligible PNs, would be permitted to expire or to be wound-down on maturity, or within a period of 5 years, whichever is earlier. Besides, reporting requirement on a regular basis has been imposed on all the FIIs.

In his 2011-12 budget speech, the Finance Minister further liberalized the portfolio investment route. He announced, "Currently, only FIIs and sub-accounts registered with the SEBI and NRIs are allowed to invest in mutual fund schemes. To liberalise the portfolio investment route, it has been decided to permit SEBI registered Mutual Funds to accept subscriptions from foreign investors who meet the KYC requirements for equity schemes. This would enable Indian mutual funds to have direct access to foreign investors and widen the class of foreign investors in Indian equity market". [2]

14.6.2 Equity Capital from Foreign Sources by Indian Corporates: Indian corporates are also allowed to access equity capital from foreign sources in the form of ADR/GDR and Euro issues. Policies on international offerings on ADRs/GDRs have been liberalised substantially and corporates are allowed to raise funds by way of ADRs/GDRs under automatic route, subject to specified guidelines.

Two-way fungibility in ADR/GDR issues of Indian companies has been introduced under which investors in India can purchase shares and deposit them with an Indian custodian for issue of ADRs/GDRs by the overseas depository to the extent of the ADRs/GDRs converted into underlying shares.

Indian corporate sector has been encouraged to access global capital markets through GDRs:

1. Foreign investors can invest in Indian companies through the GDR route without any lock-in period.
2. These receipts can be listed on any of the overseas stock exchanges and denominated in any convertible foreign currency. However, the underlying shares are denominated in Indian Rupees.
3. Private placement with US investors is also permissible in accordance with the US Securities Act.
4. Short-term capital gains are taxable at the rate of 65 percent along with business income.

5. Long-term capital gains (computed on holdings for more than 12 months) are taxable at the rate of 10 percent.

Guidelines for Euro-issues were liberalised in June 1996. The requirement of consistently good record of performance for 3 years was relaxed for companies wanting to raise GDRs or foreign currency convertible bonds (FCCBs) for financing investment in infrastructure. Restrictions on the number of issues that can be floated by an individual company or a group of companies during a financial year have been withdrawn. Earlier norms regarding end-uses of GDRs have been relaxed to include financing of import of capital goods, capital expenditure including domestic purchase/installation of plant, equipment and building, investments in software development, prepayments scheme entailing repayment of earlier external borrowings, investments abroad where these have been approved by competent authorities, and equity investment in joint ventures (JVs)/wholly owned subsidiaries (WOs) in India. A company raising GDRs can use the proceeds up to the extent of 25 percent for the purpose of meeting working capital requirements and general corporate restructuring. Furthermore, banks, financial institutions and non-banking finance companies registered with the RBI may raise GDRs without making reference to any end-uses. However, investment in the stock market and real estate is not permitted out of GDR proceeds.

GDR/ADR guidelines were further liberalised in 1998-99. Unlisted companies were permitted to float Euro issues under certain conditions. All end-use restrictions on GDR/ADR issues proceeds were removed, except the prevailing restrictions on investment in stock markets and real estate. The 90-day validity period for final approvals of GDR/ADR issues was withdrawn and final approval was continued to be valid, thereby imparting greater flexibility to issuing companies regarding the timing of issues. Indian companies were permitted to issue GDRs/ADRs in the case of bonus or right issue of shares, or on genuine business reorganisations. The companies, however, in all such cases, were required to get approval from the Department of Economic Affairs, Ministry of Finance, Government of India for the issue of GDRs/ADRs.

Considering the enhanced opportunities of Indian software companies for expanding globally, operational norms—governing their overseas investments and mode of financing acquisition of overseas software companies—were issued through a notification by the Ministry of Finance. It permitted Indian software companies, which were listed in foreign exchanges and had already floated ADR/GDR issues, to acquire foreign software companies and issue ADRs/GDRs without reference to the Government of India or the RBI up to the value limit of US$ 100 million. For acquisitions beyond US$ 100 million, proposals required examination by a Special Composite Committee in the RBI.

With a view to further liberalise the operational guidelines for ADR/GDR issues, it was decided to dispense with the track record scrutiny process for ADR/GDR issues and the two-stage approval by the Ministry of Finance. Indian companies were allowed to access the ADR/GDR markets through an automatic route without the prior approval of the Ministry of Finance subject to the specified norms and post-issue reporting requirement.

Furthermore, overseas business acquisitions through the ADR/GDR route were permitted under the automatic or simplified approval mechanism for Indian companies engaged in: (a) information technology and entertainment software; (b) pharmaceuticals; (c) biotechnology and (d) any other sector as notified by the Government from time to time. The automatic approvals was made subject to conditions of previous listing, conformation to FDI policy and limiting of transactions to US$ 100 million or ten times the export earnings during the preceding financial year. Indian companies, engaged in IT software and IT services, were permitted to issue ADR/GDR linked stock options to permanent employees (including Indian and overseas working directors) of its subsidiary companies incorporated in India or outside and engaged in IT software and IT services.

In order to encourage greater skill development in knowledge-based Indian firms, Indian companies engaged in information technology and entertainment software, pharmaceuticals, biotechnology, and any other activities within the knowledge-based sector were permitted to issue ESOPs (Employees' Stock Options) to their permanent employees. The liberalised norms for ESOPs were extended to multi-product diversified companies subject to specific conditions.

Government continued its policy of liberalising the guidelines for issue of GDRs/ADRs in a phased manner. The initiatives taken in 2001-02 included the following:

1. As a follow up of the announcement in the Budget for 2001-02, Indian companies were permitted to list in foreign stock exchanges by sponsoring ADR/GDR issues with overseas depository against shares held by its shareholders subject to prescribed conditions.
2. All companies that had made an ADR/GDR issue earlier and listed abroad were permitted the facility of overseas business acquisition through ADR/GDR stock swap under the automatic route subject to conditions that included adherence to FDI policy and the value limit for the transaction not to exceed US$ 100 million or 10 times the export earnings during the proceeding financial year.

Endnotes

1. While permitting foreign corporates/high net worth individuals in February 2000 to invest through SEBI registered FII/domestic fund managers, it was noted that there was a clear distinction between portfolio investment and FDI. The basic presumption is that FIIs are not interested in management control. To allay fears of management control being exercised by portfolio investors, it was noted that adequate safety nets were in force, for example: (a) transactions of business in securities on the stock exchanges are only through stock brokers who have been granted a certificate by SEBI, (b) every transaction is settled through a custodian who is under obligation to report to SEBI and RBI for

all transactions on a daily basis, (c) provisions of SEBI's Substantial Acquisition of Shares and Takeovers Regulations, 1997 and (d) monitoring of sectoral caps by RBI on a daily basis.

2. Government of India, Ministry of Finance, *Budget Speech of the Union Finance Minister,* 2011-12.

15

Mutual Funds in Indian Stock Market

An investment is an allocation of resources into an asset or group of assets with the expectation of generating future income or appreciation in value (e.g. investments in land, business enterprises etc.). A large number of people invest in the stock market through mutual funds or direct trading in stocks.

15.1 Meaning and Advantages of a Mutual Fund

A mutual fund is a mechanism for pooling resources by issuing units to the investors and investing funds in securities in accordance with objectives as disclosed in offer documents. Investments in securities are spread across a wide cross-section of industries and sectors and thus the risk is reduced. Diversification reduces the overall risk because all stocks may not move in the same direction or in the same proportion at the same time.

A mutual fund is a collective investment vehicle that pools together investor money. This collective pool of money is invested in accordance with a stated objective. Mutual funds are a large pool of resources managed by professionals and invested in a diverse portfolio to optimize returns for a given level of risk.

Mutual funds issue units to the investors in accordance with the quantum of money invested by them. Investors of mutual funds are known as unit holders.

Mutual funds are normally started with a number of schemes with different investment objectives that are launched from time to time. A mutual fund is required to be registered with the Securities and Exchange Board of India (SEBI) which regulates securities markets before it can collect funds from the public.

Mutual funds are very popular all over the world and they play an important role in the financial system of many countries. Mutual funds are an ideal medium for investment by small investors in the stock market. Mutual funds pool together the investments of small investors for participation in the stock market. Being institutional investors, mutual funds can afford market analysis generally not available to individual investors. Furthermore, mutual funds can diversify the portfolio in a better way as compared with individual investors due to the expertise and availability of funds.

Mutual funds have the following advantages:

1. Portfolio diversification.
2. Professional management.
3. Reduction/diversification of risk.
4. Flexibility and convenience.
5. Liquidity.
6. Reduction in transaction cost.
7. Safety of regulated environment.
8. Return potential and other benefits.

15.2 Legal and Regulatory Framework

In general, the mutual fund regulatory framework in India is much more extensive and developed than in many other countries. Indian mutual funds are unit trusts, formed under the Indian Trusts Act of 1882. Their operation is governed by mutual fund regulations, totalling 78, promulgated by SEBI in exercise of the powers conferred by Section 30, read with clause (c) of sub-section (2) of Section 11 of the Securities and Exchange Board of India, Act 1992. The first set of mutual fund regulations was originally promulgated in 1996, and has since been amended from time to time. In order to remove any difficulties in the application or interpretation of these regulations, Regulation 77 of the mutual funds regulations additionally authorises SEBI to issue "clarifications and guidelines in the form of notes or circulars which shall be binding upon the sponsor, mutual funds, trustees, asset management companies and custodians".

15.3 Operations of a Mutual Fund

Various operations of a mutual fund are shown in Figure 15.1.

Figure 15.1: Various Operations of a Mutual Fund

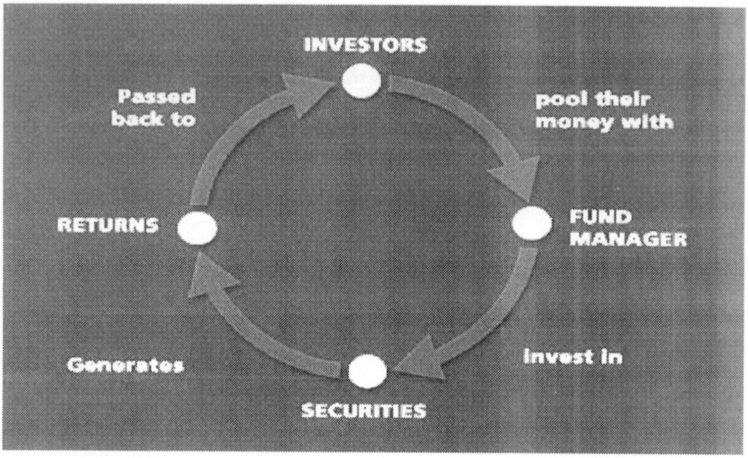

15.4 Organisation of Mutual Fund

A mutual fund is set up in the form of a trust which has the following entities:

1. Sponsor.
2. Trustees.
3. Asset Management Company (AMC).
4. Custodian.

Figure 15.2 shows the organisation of a mutual fund.

15.5 History of Mutual Funds

Mutual funds in India were first created in 1963 when the Unit Trust of India (UTI), a state-sponsored entity, came into being. Until 1987, UTI was the only mutual fund in the country. Between 1987 and 1993, other entities belonging to the public sector were permitted to offer mutual funds—basically state-controlled banks and insurers. As part of financial sector reforms, the mutual fund industry was opened to the private sector in 1993. Thus, from 1993 onwards, private sector organisations were permitted to enter the market and the first mutual fund regulations were promulgated, which were subsequently replaced by the SEBI (Mutual Fund) Regulations of 1996. These private sector organisations comprised both Indian and foreign joint ventures as well as purely Indian firms.

Figure 15.2 Organisation of a Mutual Fund

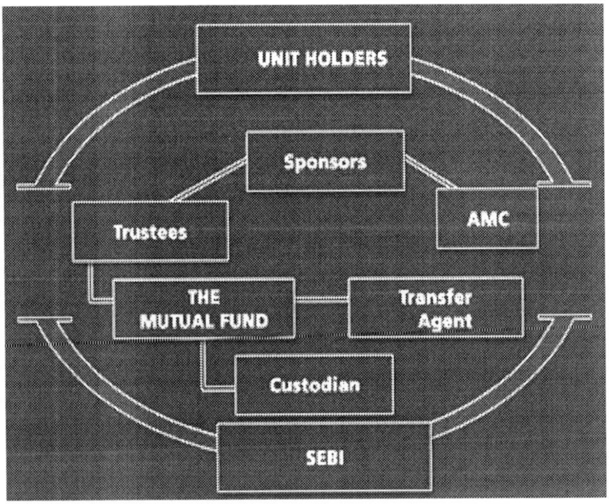

Since then, the expansion of mutual fund business has intensified competition and led to product innovation. Mutual funds presently offer a variety of options to investors such as income funds, balanced funds, liquid funds, gift funds, index funds, exchange traded funds, sectoral funds etc. The deceleration in the growth of mutual funds in the 1990s could be attributed partly to the relatively poor performance of the stock markets and partly due to withdrawal of tax benefits under Section 80M of the Indian Income Tax Act, 1961. Some of the mutual funds had offered assured return schemes enabling them to mobilise large resources. A number of mutual funds faced difficulties in meeting their redemption obligations relating to such schemes. In several cases, the sponsors of mutual funds had to infuse additional funds to meet the shortfall. As a result, mutual funds, by and large, discontinued the floatation of assured return schemes, which had some dampening effect on the resource mobilisation by mutual funds.

15.5.1 Bifurcation of UTI: While most of the mutual funds were somehow able to meet their commitments on account of assured return schemes, UTI faced a somewhat different problem on two different occasions between October 1998 and July 2001. US-64, which was the flagship scheme of UTI and enjoyed the investors' faith, first faced problem in December 1998 when the reserves under the scheme were reported negative. In order to restore investors' confidence, several measures were initiated by the Government/UTI. While these measures helped the US-64 to make a turnaround, the problem resurfaced again in July 2001 when UTI slashed down the dividend rates for the year 2000-01 and suspended sales and repurchases of US-64 for a period of 6 months from July 2001 to December 2001. This created a crisis of confidence and to restore investors' confidence various measures were initiated again, which culminated in splitting the UTI into two parts.

On October 28, 2002, an ordinance was promulgated which repealed the UTI Act, and bifurcated UTI into two separate entities. One is the Specified Undertaking of the Unit Trust of India. The Specified Undertaking of Unit Trust of India, functioning under an administrator and under the rules framed by Government of India and does not come under the purview of the mutual fund regulations. It has US-64 and the assured returns schemes. The second is the UTI Mutual Fund Ltd, sponsored by State Bank of India (SBI), Bank of Baroda (BoB), Punjab National Bank (PNB) and Life Insurance Corporation of India (LIC). It is registered with SEBI and functions under the mutual fund regulations. It is an unencumbered mutual fund, with only NAV-based schemes.

The problem with US-64 scheme of UTI adversely affected the resource mobilisation by mutual funds in general and UTI in particular. On both the occasions, when UTI faced difficulties and while resource mobilisation by UTI declined sharply, private sector mutual funds were able to fill the gap created by UTI only partially as overall mobilisation by all mutual funds on both the occasions declined sharply after the occurrence of the problem.

In March 2002, guidelines were issued to enable mutual funds to invest in rated securities in countries with fully convertible currencies. This marked an important milestone, through which mutual funds will be able to deliver better risk/return tradeoffs through international diversification.

15.6 Features of Mutual Fund Industry in India

These are as under:

1. Mutual funds are popular mainly with the middle and high-income groups.
2. Investors are largely based in the urban centres, particularly the metropolitan cities.
3. Penetration of mutual funds in the rural areas remains small.
4. UTI and other state-owned asset management companies have lost market share, while private sector funds have grown rapidly.
5. Asset management companies are divided into those that are predominantly owned by the state (UTI, bank sponsored and institutions) and those that are in the private sector.
6. Mutual fund industry has to compete with attractive assured returns from Government schemes and this is possibly the single most important impediment to the growth of the industry.

Thus, if mutual funds have to grow fast, they would need to devise appropriate schemes to attract the saving of low-income groups, especially in rural areas. This is the only way to ensure participation of all categories of investors into the capital market, which is so crucial for its long-term development.

15.7 Types of Mutual Funds

Mutual funds can be classified as under:

15.7.1 Open-ended Funds:

1. Units are available for sale/purchase at all times at NAV based prices.
2. Fresh subscriptions may be discontinued.
3. Unit capital is variable.
4. Redemptions at any time is allowed, except when there is lock-in period

15.7.2 Close-ended Funds:

1. Initial public offer (IPO).
2. Investor cannot buy units later on from mutual fund.
3. Unit capital remains constant.
4. Redemption of units on expiry date.
5. Traded on stock exchange at a discount to NAV.
6. Buyback of units' option may be allowed.

15.7.3 Load Funds: Load is one time fee payable by the investor when he enters/exists from the funds. Loads are charged to recover initial issue expenses including marketing and selling expenses, brokerage, advertising costs etc. There can be entry load or exit load or both.

15.7.4 No-load Funds: In a no-load fund, marketing and selling expenses are not imposed on the investors. An investor buys and sells units at net asset value (NAV).

15.7.5 Growth/Equity Oriented Funds: The aim of growth funds is to provide capital appreciation over the medium and long-term. Such schemes normally invest a major part of their corpus in equities. They have comparatively high risks.

15.7.6 Income/Debt Oriented Funds: The aim of income funds is to provide regular and steady income to investors. Such schemes generally invest in fixed income securities such as bonds, corporate debentures, government securities and money market instruments. Such funds are less risky compared to equity schemes.

15.7.7 Tax-exempt Funds: Mutual funds invested in government or municipal bonds are often referred to as tax-free or tax-exempt funds because the interest generated by these bonds is not subject to income tax. However, not all bonds are exempt from all taxes.

15.7.8 Non-tax Exempt Funds: Mutual funds invested in bonds the interest from which is subject to income tax, can be called non-tax exempt mutual funds.

15.8 Problems of Mutual Funds

India has a high household savings ratio. Indians, like most people anywhere, are conservative in their habits, and it would take many years to change this behaviour, particularly when it comes to the use of their savings. As in most countries, investment in physical assets (mainly housing and gold) accounts for the most important percentage of household assets. Owning a home is usually a first priority once a family has any disposable income at all.

15.8.1 Competition with Government Schemes: Mutual funds compete against a host of high yielding government-backed savings schemes such as public provident fund (PPF), national savings scheme (NSS), RBI bonds, and so on, as well as against life insurance products and, in the future, against the new pension schemes for the unorganised sector. [1] The political and social reasons for keeping yields higher than the market for small savers, particularly retired savers, is understandable. The market is distorted by such a policy. Government should have the strategic aim of discontinuing over time or at least reducing the availability of the unrealistically high yielding avenues for small savings. The objective of widening and deepening ownership of mutual funds is unlikely to be met until this happens.

Fixed income and balanced mutual funds have offered a

reasonably competitive rate of return but they are not guaranteed, a key attraction to Indian investors. The net result is that mutual funds fail to attract much money from retail investors, who prefer to invest in a no-risk, high return product, i.e. government saving schemes or provident funds or keep their money safely in the bank.

Government-sponsored instruments *crowd out* mutual funds since for the majority of Indians buying mutual funds, before they have their full complement of government-backed savings instruments, would be both wrong and foolish.

In most countries government guaranteed financial instruments offer returns that are likely to be significantly lower than private sector investments available from mutual funds or insurance companies. This is the penalty that investors are prepared to pay for little or no risk. However, Indian retail investors are not being asked to sacrifice any substantial amount of return in exchange for a government guarantee. Conversely, returns on government assured investments are often better than those available elsewhere. While conventional government bonds do give lower returns than equivalent private sector corporate bonds, the retail government assured products give higher returns for almost no risk. It is thus hardly surprising that an investor of modest means would choose to invest in, for instance, national savings certificates, since he can thus obtain a better return for a much lower risk. Any investor would be well advised to invest the maximum permitted in the various government assured schemes before considering other forms of investment.

The reasons why the government is prepared to pay above market rates of interest on certain financial products is understandable. At a time when interest rates have fallen substantially from their previous levels, savers who had counted on the interest on their savings to provide an income, particularly in retirement, are being subsidised. Given that pension arrangements, particularly in the unorganised sector, are not widespread, such an approach is reasonable and indeed most small savers are acting rationally when they choose the low risk option. However, this approach conflicts with a desire to widen and deepen participation in capital markets through mutual funds or other non-governmental savings products by the less well-off sectors of the population.

15.8.2 Competition from Insurance: The take up life assurance is growing rapidly and may be pre-empting some of the market that mutual funds could aim at. Life assurance is an easier product to sell, since in the mind of the investor the payment of a premium is often linked to a specific outcome, a lump sum payment on death or a guaranteed minimum sum on maturity. It also pays higher commissions to sales agents (typically the amount of the first 5 to 6 months premium). Thus, a sales agent will usually prefer to sell a life policy since it will reward him better.

15.8.3 Volatility of Mutual Fund Performance: There is a perception that mutual funds have somehow let down their investors and given them poor returns. In July 2001 when UTI slashed down the dividend rates for the year 2000-01 and suspended sales and repurchases of US-64 for a period of 6 months from July 2001 to December 2001, it created a crisis of confidence among the investors with long-term effects.

15.8.4 Tax System Encourages Short-term Objectives: Mutual funds are regarded in most countries as a diversified, professionally managed and well-regulated vehicle for mobilising household savings and are often accorded tax privileges specifically in pursuit of a government policy goal to encourage long-term savings, notably for retirement. [2] It is unusual for such tax privileges to impel mutual funds towards short-term goals, which is what seems to be the case in India. True, Indian unit trusts are diversified, professionally managed and well-regulated, but they are certainly not serving long-term objectives.

15.9 Mutual Funds and the Stock Market

Mutual funds in India, because of their small size and slower growth in the recent past, have tended to play only a limited role in the stock market. In view of small size of their operations, mutual funds in normal times hardly exert any influence on the stock market. Mutual funds with large funds at their disposal are expected by the government to act as a counterweight to foreign institutional investors (FIIs), which generally exert a significant influence on the stock market. Some leading asset management companies in India are listed in Table 15.1.

Table 15.1: Leading Asset Management Companies in India

S. No.	Name of the Company
Bank Sponsored	
1.	Baroda BNP Paribas Asset Management Ind Pvt. Ltd.
2.	Canara Robeco Asset Management Co. Ltd.
3.	SBI Funds Management Pvt. Ltd.
4.	Union Asset Management Co. Pvt. Ltd.
5.	Bank of India Investment Managers Pvt. Ltd.
6.	IDBI Asset Management Ltd.
7.	UTI Asset Management Co. Ltd.
Institutions	
1.	IIFCL Asset Management Co. Ltd.
2.	LIC Mutual Fund Asset Management Ltd.
Private Sector (Indian and Foreign)	
1.	DSP Investment Managers Pvt. Ltd.
2.	Edelweiss Asset Management Ltd.
3.	Franklin Templeton Asset Management (India) Pvt. Ltd.
4.	HSBC Asset Management (India) Pvt. Ltd.
5.	IDFC Asset Management Co. Ltd.
6.	IIFL Asset Management Ltd.
7.	IL&FS Infra Asset Management Ltd.
8.	Indiabulls Asset Management Co. Ltd.
9.	Invesco Asset Management (India) Pvt. Ltd.
10.	ITI Asset Management Ltd.
11.	JM Financial Asset Management Ltd.
12.	Kotak Mahindra Asset Management Co. Ltd.
13.	L&T Investment Management Ltd.
14.	Motilal Oswal Asset Management Co. Ltd.
15.	Mirae Asset Investment Managers (India) Pvt. Ltd.
16.	Navi AMC Ltd.

17.	NJ Asset Management Pvt. Ltd.
18.	Nippon Life India Asset Management Ltd.
19.	PGIM India Asset Management Pvt. Ltd.
20.	PPFAS Asset Management Pvt. Ltd.
21.	Quant Money Managers Ltd.
22.	Quantum Asset Management Co. Pvt. Ltd.
23.	Samco Asset Management Pvt. Ltd.
24.	Shriram Asset Management Co. Ltd.
25.	Sundaram Asset Management Co. Ltd.
26.	Tata Asset Management Pvt. Ltd.
27.	Taurus Asset Management Co. Ltd.
28.	Trust Asset Management Management Pvt. Ltd.
29.	WhiteOak Capital Asset Management Ltd.
Joint Ventures (Indian and Foreign)	
1.	Aditya Birla Sun Life AMC Ltd.
2.	Axis Asset Management Co. Ltd.
3.	HDFC Asset Management Co. Ltd.
4.	ICICI Prudential Asset Management Co. Ltd.
5.	Mahindra Manulife Investment Management Pvt. Ltd.

15.10 Measures to Evaluate Portfolio Performance

Table 15.2 shows some of classic and widely-used measures of portfolio performance.

Table 15.2: Some Classic and Widely-used Measures of Portfolio Performance

Measure	Meaning	Formula	Applications
Sharpe Ratio	It is measure for calculating risk adjusted returns. It uses standard deviation (σ) to measure risk (volatility)	It is calculated by subtracting risk free rate (R_f) from the mean returns per standard deviation (R) $SR=\frac{R-Rf}{\sigma}$ Where $\sigma = Standard\ deviaion$	A higher Sharpe ratio is better– reflecting higher returns

contd...

Treynor Ratio	It is similar to Sharpe ratio, but it is a risk adjusted measure of returns, based on systematic risk	This ratio uses beta (β) as the measure of risk (Volatility) $TR = \frac{R-(Rf)}{\beta}$	A higher Treynor Ratio is better
Jensen's Alpha	It is the expected return on the portfolio, adjusted for the return earned for taking market risk	It measures performance as the excess return provided by portfolio over the (CAPM) returns $(R) = R_f - \beta(R_m - R_f)$ Where, R= Expected returns R_f= Risk free rate of returns Rm= Market rate of returns B= Beta JA= R- (R)	The larger the alpha better it is

To sum up, the mutual fund industry in India is quite sophisticated and successful. It is dominated by good and reputable institutions, both Indian and foreign. Nevertheless, improvements are always possible and desirable in order to enhance the ability of the mutual fund industry to mobilise savings on a wider scale and to contribute to the further development of capital market.

Endnotes

1. Many of the government assured schemes are probably not fulfilling their original purpose. For example, the Public Provident Fund (PPP) was set up in 1968-69 with the objective of providing unorganised sector workers with a facility to accumulate savings for old age income security. As a result of premature withdrawal facilities and tax breaks, individuals largely misuse this scheme for legitimised tax evasion and it does not serve the intended purpose of old age income security.
2. There is no perfect system for taxing the income and gains of mutual funds and their investors. The main principle that almost all regimes follow is that there should be broadly equality of treatment between all mutual fund investors and between mutual fund

investors and direct investors in securities. In other words, an investor purchasing assets indirectly through a mutual fund should be no worse off tax-wise than if that same investor bought those assets directly on their own behalf. This is the principle of *fiscal neutrality*.

The taxation of funds is a key issue for funds and their management companies. Taxation affects both the attractiveness of funds compared with other investments, and also the systems that may have to be designed and implemented in order for funds to operate efficiently and cost effectively. Fund managers in virtually every market in the world lobby governments hard either to remove tax disadvantages or to achieve favourable treatment, so that their product can become more competitive in the market and more attractive to potential buyers.

Bibliography

Bibliography

Books

Agashe, Anil (2007), "Capital Market and Financial Services", Everest Publishing House, Mumbai.

Agrawal, Krishna Kumar (1997), "Capital Market in India", Anmol Publication, Pvt. Ltd., New Delhi.

Alagiri, Dhandapani and Sabari, Ganesh (2006), "Securitization", ICFAI University Press, Hyderabad.

B.J. Queensly, Jayanthi (2010), "A Study on National Stock Exchange of India", Serials Publication, New Delhi.

Banerjee, Arindam (2006), "Indian Capital Market", ICFAI University Press, Hyderabad.

Berman, H.D. (1962), "The Stock Exchanges", Pitman Publishing, Ltd.

Bhasin, Niti (2014), "Indian Financial System: Evolution and Present Structure", New Century Publications, New Delhi.

Bhatia, B. (1978), "New Issue Market of India", Vora and Co. Publishers Pvt. Ltd.

Board of Editors (2004), "Securities Markets and Instruments", ICFAI University Press, Hyderabad.

Chakraborty, Tanupa (2008), "Buyback of Shares in India", New Century Publications, New Delhi.

Chakravarti, Lata (2005), "Foreign Direct Investment in India", IFCAI University Press, Hyderabad.

Chaudhari, Tamal Datta (2006), "Financial Sector Reforms", ICFAI Publication, Hyderabad.

Cliff, Prate (1994), "The Stock Market", Cambridge University Press.

Fabozzi, Frank J. and Modigliani, Franco (2007), "Capital Markets Institutions and Instruments", Prentice Hall of India Pvt. Ltd., New Delhi.

Ghosh, Rajarshi (2005), "Foreign Direct Investment Policies and Experience", ICFAI University Press, Hyderabad.

Gorden, E. and Natraj, K. (1999), "Capital Market in India",

Himalaya Publishing House, Mumbai.
Gordon, E. and Natarajan, K. (2009), "Financial Markets and Financial Services", Himalaya Publishing House, Mumbai.
Gupta, L.C. (1997), "India's Stock Market Crisis", Society for Capital Market Research and Development.
Gupta, Saloni (2010), "Stock Market in India", New Century Publications, New Delhi.
Jadhav, R.K. (1991), "Development of Capital Market in India", A.J. Enterprise, Mumbai.
Kaur, Harvindar (2002), "Stock Market Volatility in India", Deep and Deep Publications Pvt. Ltd., New Delhi.
Khan, Javed (2005), "Operation of Stock Exchange in India", Vista International Publishing House, New Delhi.
Khan, M.Y. (1978), "New Issue Market and Finance for Industry in India", Allied Publisher Pvt. Ltd., New Delhi.
Khatri, D.K. (2006), "Investment Management and Securities Analysis", Macmillan India Ltd., New Delhi.
Komaromi, Gyorgy (2006), "Anatomy of Stock Market Bubbles", ICFAI Publication University Press, Hyderabad.
Lahiri, Sandip and Pain, Asis Kumar (2006), "Indian Stock Market", ICFAI Press, Hyderabad.
Machiraju, H.R. (2009), "The Working of Stock Exchange in India", New Age International Publisher, New Delhi.
Machiraju, H.R. (2008), "Indian Financial System", Vikas Publishing House Ltd., Noida.
Madhusoodanan, T.P. (2006), "Indian Capital Markets: Theory and Empirical Evidence", Unit Trust of India, Mumbai.
Mishra, Bhanupriya and Debasish, Sathya Swaroop (2008), "Indian Stock Market", Excel Books, New Delhi.
Mittal, Anand (2003), "Economic Reforms and Capital Market in India", Galgotia Publishing Company Ltd., New Delhi.
Pain, Asis Kumar (2007), "Financial Sector and Economic Growth Linkage", ICFAI University Press, Hyderabad.
Pathak, Bharat V. (2006), "Indian Financial System", Dorling Kindersley, (India) Pvt. Ltd., New Delhi.
Pullani, Ravi and Pullani, Mahesh (2010), "Manual of SEBI:

Act, Rules, Regulations, Circulars", Volume I, Bharat Law House Pvt. Ltd., New Delhi.

Raghunathan, V. (1991), "Stock Exchanges and Investments", Tata McGraw Hill Publishing Company Ltd., New Delhi.

Sehgal, Sanjay (2005), "Asset Pricing in Indian Stock Market", New Century Publication, New Delhi.

Sharma, A.K, and Batra, G.S. (2000), "Indian Stock Market", Elegant Printer, New Delhi.

Singh, Joginder (1994), "Working of a Security Market in India", Reliance Publishing House, New Delhi.

Singh, Preeti (2009), "Dynamics of Indian Financial System Markets, Institutions and Services", Ane Book Pvt. Ltd., New Delhi.

Sridhar, A.N. (2008), "Future and Options", Shroff Publishers and Distributors Pvt. Ltd., Mumbai.

Tadashi, Endo (1998), "The Indian Securities Market", Vision Books, New Delhi.

Torre, Augnsto De La and Sehmukler, Sergio L. (2007), "Emerging Capital Markets and Globalisation: Latin American Experience", Stanford University Press and World Bank.

Venkatash, T.R. (ed.) (2004), "Indian Financial Market", ICFAI University Press, Hyderabad.

Research Articles

Barua, S.K., Raghunathan V. and Verma J.R. (1994), "Research on the Indian Capital Market: A Review", *Vikalpa*, January-March, Volume 19, No. 1.

Bose, Suchismita and Mukherjee, Parmita (2005), "A Study of Inter-linkages Between Indian Stock Market and Some Other Emerging and Developed Market", *World Economic Outlook,* IMF, April.

Choudhary, Neelam, Gupta, Gitanjali and Gupta, Anand (2010), "Impact of FII Investment on Indian Stock Market and Research", *Indian Journal of Commerce*, Volume 63, October-December.

Gangadhar, V. and Reddy, G. Naresh (2009), "Stock Market Volatility: Analysis of NSE and BSE", *Finance India*, Volume XXIII, No. 4, December.

Kelkar, Vijay (2011), "Moving Ahead with Exchange Reforms", NSE working paper series, available at: http:// www.nseindia.com.

Mishra, P.K. and Malla, M. (2010), "Performance of Indian Capital Market: An Empirical Analysis", *European Journal of Economics, Finance and Administrative Sciences*, Issue 23.

Mishra, P.K. and Das, K.B. (2009), "Role of FIIs in Indian Capital Market", *The Research Network*, Volume 4, No. 2.

Nagraj. R. (1996), "India's Capital Market Growth: Trends, Explanations and Evidences", *Economic and Political Weekly*, Volume XXXI, Nos. 35, 36 and 37.

Pandey, Ajay (2005), "Volatility Models and their Performance in Indian Capital Markets", *Vikalpa*, Volume 30, No. 2, April -June.

Pandian, Punithavathy and Queensly, Jayanthi, (2009), "Stock Market Volatility in Indian Stock Exchanges", available at: www.Indiastat.com,www.indiastat.com/article /05/punit/fulltext.pdf - United States.

Sabarinathan, G. (2010), "SEBI's Regulation of the Indian Securities Market: A Critical Review of the Major Development", *Vikalpa*, Volume 35, No.4, October-December.

Samarita, G.P. and Patak, Rajashree (2001), "On Construction of a Composite Indicator for Predicting Stock Prices in India", *Finance India*, Volume XV, No. 2.

Sarma, S.N. (2004), "Stock Market Seasonality in an Emerging Market", *Vikalpa*, Volume 29, No. 3, July-September.

Sharma, J.C. (2002), "Do Indian Stock Prices Follow Random Walk? An Enquiry", *Asian Economic Review*.

Singh, Narendra Bohara and Dutta, Akash (2011), "Foreign

Institutional Investment in Indian Capital Market", *International Research of Finance and Economics*, Issue 68, pp. 1450-2887, available at: http://eurojournals .com/finance.htm.

Udegbunam, Ralph I. and Eriki, P.O. (2001), "Inflation and Stock Market Behaviour: Evidence from Nigerian Stock Market", *Journal of Financial Management of Analysis,* Volume 14 No. 1, January-June.

Reports and Government Publications

Annual Reports of BSE (various years)
Annual Reports of SEBI (various years)
Handbook of Statistics on the Indian Securities Market (SEBI)
Report on Currency and Finance (RBI) (various years)
BSE: Stock Exchange Reviews

Webliography

www.bseindia.com
www.nseindia.com
www.rbi.org.in
www.sebi.gov.in

Index

Index